Motivate Yourself and Reach Your Goals

Frances Coombes

Frances Coombes is an NLP Master Practitioner, life coach and motivational trainer. She runs 'Callings' coaching and support groups for people in transition through work and life. She runs NLP courses at City Lit, London and independently, currently working with an NHS Foundation Trust's recovery support team, and with children in schools, developing people's skills, confidence, self-esteem and personal growth.

The theory behind this book

This book contains many of Richard Bandler's neuro-linguistic programming (NLP) techniques, which are a set of tools designed to give people as many choices as possible around how they make decisions, increase their motivation and take action.

I developed the book over ten years running NLP courses for diverse groups of people. On weekly courses, people monitored their behaviour, their motivation and outcomes, so that the results they achieved were evidence-based. People's stories may be different but many of the things they want are similar: confidence, motivation, self-esteem, to have options, a plan and a strong sense of purpose in life and to overcome the anxieties that hold them back.

NLP presupposes that people can be taught positive skills that will interact with each other so that that the person's whole way of experiencing life can be transformed – as the book explains, 'like lining your ducks in a row'. The techniques seek to restore a sense of control, choice, motivation and mastery to people – opening options for new, more positive behaviours.

The aim of NLP and this book is to create the richest map possible for you by enlarging the choices that you perceive as being available to you in the world.

Teach Yourself®

Motivate Yourself and Reach Your Goals

Frances Coombes

Contents

1

What drives motivation and performance?

In this chapter you will:

► *Explore the tools and techniques you want to acquire*

► *Identify how you can use strategies for your own purpose*

► *Tune into how others are viewing the world*

► *Design a metaphor that gives you more choices in life*

► *Test the evidence to make sure your strategies work for you.*

'It's all in line'

'In line, in line, it's all in line. My ducks are all in a row...'
James Taylor, American singer-songwriter

Life becomes simpler when you know your purpose and have a model and some simple tried-and-tested principles to work to. In this book you will find tools to help you discover your beliefs, values, goals, motivation and purpose in life. You are learning to line your ducks in a row, as the James Taylor song puts it, by simplifying and aligning your thoughts, beliefs and behaviours, so that they flow together to make all your efforts work for you.

Making quick and lasting changes for the better becomes easy once you harness the power of your motivation – and use it. Imagine how immensely powerful you will feel when your thoughts, beliefs and actions are aligned and you are already achieving the things that you want to on a regular basis. You may want to...

► start your own business

► increase your sales by overcoming your fear of making cold calls

► get a better job

► change disempowering beliefs that hold you back.

Once you have a framework to work to and some simple processes to follow, you can visualize and define your goals more effectively. When you can clearly visualize the outcomes you want, and taste the emotions of success in advance, new options spring up to encourage you to turn your goals into reality.

This book will help you to set and surpass your expectations by drawing on a wealth of life-changing tools and adapting them to suit your needs. The book will give you the tools to identify the characteristics of successful achievers so that you can model their success strategies and make them your own. Undertaking the exercises will enable you to identify more fully how you can unlock your potential, surpass your expectations of what you think you can achieve, and improve your effectiveness in every aspect of your life.

An overview

The techniques we will use may seem simple, but they build into a very powerful model for achieving more of the things you want to in life. In the case study below I have quoted extensively from a magazine article I wrote that includes many of the topics we will cover and that demonstrates how others are already using the skills to achieve their aims. Reading this will give you a flavour of the tools you can expect to use and the kind of situations you might find them useful in. Afterwards, I will ask you to list the techniques that seem useful to you – look out for the corresponding exercises throughout the book.

Case study: Give people the strategies they want

Recently, I ran an in-house training day for a mixed group of hospital staff. Learners agreed that a successful outcome for the day would be to go away with at least three or four really good strategies they could take away and use to feel more confident in their working and personal lives. The group also wanted strategies that would equip them to address problems that were at the forefront of their minds at that moment. Based on the requirements of the group, we chose strategies from the following Neuro-linguistic Programming (NLP) toolkit.

EXAMPLES OF HOW TOOLS ARE USED

1 Self-management skills

Increasingly, managers have greater numbers of staff reporting to them, and so will have minimal time allotted to developing individual employees. People who can think for themselves and can manage themselves in relation to their work and life are the ones who will do best in the modern world.

* *Strategies for focusing and clarifying and setting good outcomes.* Have a framework for thinking about outcomes: ask yourself, 'What is the goal in the actions I am taking right now? Am I moving forward or marking time? What needs to happen for change to happen? What would make things work for me?'
* *The ability to build your inner confidence by managing your internal state.* Ask yourself, 'How much do I want this outcome on a scale of 1–10? What am I assuming that is stopping me from achieving that goal? Is what I am thinking a "Fact" / "Possible Fact" / or a "Limiting Assumption"?'

* *Tools for getting yourself into the right frame of mind to do a task.* It is important to remember past victories and resources we possess and come to new situations armed with these powerful tools.
* *Setting outcomes for negotiations.* Check that you are on the same wavelength as the other parties. Summarize what has just been said. Ask yourself. 'What is the point of my message seen from the viewpoint of the other person? Are there any emerging difficulties that I did not recognize before?'
* *Dealing with things that are stressful.* Sometimes just ask: 'What is a better behaviour to have instead of the one I am using right now? What kind of beliefs may be fuelling my behaviour? What fears do I have over changing my behaviour?'

2 Building better communication skills

* Building rapport skills with others
* Understand better your own and other people's behaviours
* Noticing what motivates you/others to get things done

What made the learning attractive to participants was that they first set individual outcomes so they could have evidence-based results, and recognized that the skills they were learning for work are also transferable to all aspects of their lives. Techniques learned can be used to improve not just learners' work and career issues but also to aid their relationships with children, lovers, relatives and friends.

3 Modelling successful outcomes

If you want to be successful, find someone who already has the skills and then model them. Most people start with small individual skills and then move on to group work and greater things. Group examples of using modelling skills are:

* *Great Ormond Street Hospital theatre team* noted that they were saving patients' lives in theatre, but that the minutes between leaving the theatre and reaching high-dependency wards were critical. They modelled Formula One racing drivers' pit-stop crews responsible for refuelling a car in seconds, and then devised new rules for getting patients from A to B in the shortest possible time.
* *Eurostar* has used the NLP modelling technique to train control staff who manage the rail terminals. The aim was to find out what makes an

excellent terminal controller and give colleagues the opportunity to try out the same thinking for themselves. If one person can do a task really well, that's good. If two or three people can do it equally well, that is even better. If all staff can do it, then that is approaching excellence.

✻ *The charity Save the Children* did not have money to alleviate poverty in Vietnamese villages. Instead, the team adopted a modelling approach. They noticed that some children were better nourished than most others. The team enlisted village mums to find out what was different about the way those children were fed. Mothers discovered that healthier children were fed more often (the same amount of food but in smaller portions). Also these mothers were mixing in sources of protein that were not considered appropriate for children. By getting the rest of the mothers to model the same practices, six months later 65 per cent of the children in the village were better nourished.

4 Listening and thinking skills

Many people carry emotional baggage as a result of stress, overwork, competition, the effects of reorganization, takeover, redundancy, or doing a totally different job from the one they used to do. Keeping a 'stiff upper lip' can appear to maintain equilibrium, but people who carry emotional baggage are less able to enjoy their life or their work, or give their best efforts to it. NLP has lots of tools for helping people to get around emotional blocks in order to move forward and achieve more of what they want. When participants look back on NLP training it is usually these reflective techniques and the action-planning skills that people remember most.

The aim of teaching people NLP in work, in relationships, in life is to give everyone the widest range of options and tools that might be available to them at any time. NLP training helps enrich the choices that people perceive as being available to them in the world; it gives them powerful new techniques for their toolkit.

(Adapted from my article, 'NLP Training in the NHS Workplace', *Positive Health* magazine, issue 195, June 2012, www.positivehealth.com/author/frances-coombes/frances-coombes)

Try it now: Create a list of the tools you want to acquire

Imagine yourself in a large supermarket with lots of products on the shelves. These packages are not filled with washing power and food but are full of the qualities and skills you might like to have. As you slowly walk around and peruse the shelves, you might decide you would like to have a box of 'Confidence' and a large jar of 'Good Rapport', maybe a bottle of high-strength 'Listening Skills', a jar of 'Problem-solving Strategies' or a large tin of 'Creativity Boosters'. Gather them in your trolley and proceed to the checkout.

✳ Now, in case you have forgotten anything, glance through the case study above again.

✳ Make a list of the tools and strategies mentioned that might be useful to you when you are seeking to motivate yourself and get things done.

✳ For each new strategy, write down when you would apply them to make things happen in your own particular situation.

✳ Set aside 20 minutes to think about the situations you might use these resources for.

✳ Finally, use the following form to reflect on how you think each of your chosen techniques might be able to help you.

Name of technique:

Why would you want to acquire this technique?

What would having this technique let you do that you cannot already do as well as you would like to right now?

If others were watching you, how would they know that you had acquired this skill? What would they see, hear and feel that would tell them there was something different about you?

How motivated are you now?

If you are going on a motivational journey, it is good to check how many miles you cover by measuring the distance from where you started out from. This is just a fun exercise, but it should get you thinking about how motivated you feel right now.

Self-assessment: Check your current state of motivation

Answer the following questions, scoring yourself on a scale of 1–10 as to how motivated you feel.

1 Do you wake up each morning and hit the ground running? (___/10)

2 Are you excited about the new day and the new choices, challenges and chances you have to explore? (___/10)

3 Do you have a strong image in your mind's eye of what living successfully looks like, and feels like to you? (___/10)

4 Are you settling for a life of reasonable contentment because you don't really know what you want in life? (___/10)

5 Are you doing reasonably well, but success seems to come in fits and starts? (___/10)

6 Are you unaware of your dreams in life, and simply plod along each day? (___/10)

Giving yourself a score lets you gauge your level of engagement with the things you are doing on a daily basis. It also gives you a chance to reflect on what would need to happen to nudge your score from a 3 to an 8, or a 5 to a 9.

Your needs

Sometimes we beat ourselves up because we are not achieving all the things we think we ought to. There may be obvious reasons for what we see as our underachievement. We may need to have met certain criteria before we can think about self-fulfilment and achieving our purpose in life.

At the most basic level, these needs are food, shelter, clothes, warmth. If these needs are met, then we look for friends, self-esteem and kinship, a feeling of belonging. If all these needs are met, then some of us seek self-actualization, the chance to grow and become motivated to find and achieve a meaningful life purpose (Figure 1.1).

Figure 1.1 Maslow's hierarchy of needs

BASIC NEEDS: While your basic needs – water, food, clothes – are most likely being met, it is higher up in the pyramid that things might be missing.

SAFETY: Feeling secure, knowing you can pay the rent and that your everyday living needs are met.

BELONGING TO TRIBE: Do you have groups you feel you belong to? These might be family and friends, cultural, religious, work and hobby groups, people that make you feel that you are connected to other people.

SELF-ESTEEM: When our basic needs are met, and we belong to a tribe, we look for self-esteem. Can you remember when was the last time someone said to you: 'You did that really well – I am pleased with what you've done.' And when did you last tell someone that you were really pleased with what they had done? This is the basis for how we create and receive self-esteem.

SELF-ACTUALIZATION If our lower needs are provided for, then we have space, energy and time to think, and so the higher up the pyramid we go. We begin to wonder about what would make us happy, what we want in life, and what our purpose in life is. How do we fulfil ourselves and achieve the things that we feel passionate about and are meaningful to our lives?

Try it now: Where are you on the hierarchy of needs

Use Figure 1.1 to help you think about the following:

1 Set aside ten minutes' quiet time to reflect on where you believe you are on Maslow's hierarchy of needs.
2 Tick which of your needs are already being met.
3 Draw a line at the point you believe you are on the hierarchy of needs.
4 Describe what needs to happen for you to move up the hierarchy of needs.

What do you really want?

> 'Action may not always bring happiness, but there is no happiness without action.'
>
> Benjamin Disraeli, Victorian politician

People often say they know what they want in life and may spend their time engaged in displacement activities, only to find that, after they have swapped their job, partner or location, they have carried their feelings of discontent with them. They have changed what seemed obvious in their lives but have not identified the main changes that would make the difference to them.

Knowing who you are and discovering what you really want are key to taking actions that will propel you towards greater successes. Knowing what you want is a hard question; in fact, most people postpone the intense self-reflection and life choices necessary to create a life they want to enjoy. Often, they shrug off tackling the question at all by saying: 'I am much too busy being busy even to begin to think about how I get the life I really want.'

We can all answer the easy questions such as 'What shall I do this weekend?' or 'What shall I have for dinner?' More challenging questions are: 'What shall I do with the rest of my life?' or 'How do I live my life in a more meaningful way?'

Think about the following questions:

▶ What are the things that you are naturally drawn to?

▶ What are the things you were good at as a child

▶ What are the changes you will need to make to get the life you want?

▶ Do you already know where you are going in life and have a plan of how you will get there?

▶ Do your answers indicate you are moving in the direction you want to in life? Or are you merely marking time?

Whatever you discover is like mining for gold, so make sure you write your answers down.

If you don't know where you are going, then any road will take you there, because it will be wherever you accidently end up. You need to set goals with lots of milestones on the way to check how on target you are towards achieving your dreams.

> 'The first principle is that you must not fool yourself, and you are the easiest person to fool.'
> Richard P. Feynman, Nobel Prize-winning physicist

Taking control

We control our lives, and create the contents of our lives anew each day – which is essentially what Henry Ford meant when he said: 'If you think you can, or you think you can't, you are right.' We create a life of self-fulfilling prophecy, which can be fantastic if we have a positive mindset, but disastrous if we have a negative view of our capacity to get the things we want in life.

With each thought we think, and habitual thinking pattern we run, we deepen the grooves of our optimistic or pessimistic outlook on life. Our thoughts, emotions, habits and the actions we take, or fail to take, have brought us to where we are today.

Some people settle for a reasonable level of contentment and give up on striving for the big dreams in life. Others believe that whatever happens is meant to be; they hand over a lot of their power and ability to make things happen to a force that is outside of themselves.

Some people recognize their lives could be better, if only they could get their act together and build a structured plan to work to. Others stay exactly where they are and don't advance towards their dreams because they believe that they are not worthy or don't have any control over life.

The truth is that you do have control over your life; you are controlling it every day. Even doing nothing is a decision-making strategy – it helps us to stay where we are and not take any risks. There are three ways that decisions are made: either you make them; someone else makes them for you, or time passes and the opportunity is gone.

Knowing where you are on the 'Cause and Effect Continuum' is a very powerful learning exercise. Although the insights you may take from it are not always comfortable, they are the basis for changing your behaviour, taking risks and moving on in life. Look at the following diagram, then try the exercise that follows.:

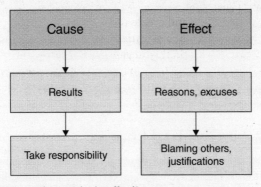

Figure 1.2 Are you 'at cause' or 'at effect'?

Try it now: Which side of the 'Cause and Effect Continuum' are you on?

Are you on the 'Cause' side where you take responsibility for everything that is happening in your life, or are you on the 'Effect' side where you blame others and offer reasons and excuses and justifications for why the things that you attempted did not work? Attitude is what it is about, and is what makes things happen. This is about you taking responsibility for everything that happens in your universe.

Think back to the last three times when things went wrong for you, and consider the following:

* Did you blame other people, or circumstances for what happened? Or did you take responsibility for what happened?
* If you blamed others, list the reasons, excuses, justifications you used.
* Is there a pattern to your behaviour in all three events?
* What does that pattern of behaviour tell you about which side of the 'Cause and Effect Continuum' you function on?

Using the insight this has given you, use the following action plan to help you gain maximum power and to take responsibility for all that happens in your world. Take charge of your life and decide how you will bring about the changes you want to happen.

* Focus on one thing you want to accomplish at a time, until you become expert.
* Make a plan for how you will do it and the steps along the way.
* Chunk big tasks down into bite-sized pieces, and tackle one piece at a time.
* Visualize your goal as already having been achieved and you feeling happy and congratulating yourself because it is all done.
* Think about what having this goal might do for you – might it give you leverage to achieve another goal?

What I wish I had known

When we fail to achieve our desires, often with hindsight we can see that it is because we wanted to play safe, not take risks, concentrate on day-to-day living, and not allow ourselves to dream. We are like children building sandcastles on a beach – there is no sense of time or urgency until someone says 'OK, it's time to go!' and we realize that we haven't had long enough to fulfil all our dreams.

A magazine survey of people in their eighties which asked the question 'If you had your life over again, what would you do differently?' revealed that the majority of people expressed three really important wishes that they did not allow themselves to fulfil during their lifetimes:

▶ 'I wish I had let myself be happier.'

▶ 'I wish I had had the courage to truly express myself.'

▶ 'I wish I had lived true to my dreams, instead of what others expected of me.'

No one said 'I wish I had worried more' or 'I wish I had watched more TV'. Regrets were mostly for what they had *not* done. When asked more specifically what they would do differently, top of the list came:

▶ 'I would focus more on my values and larger goals and not be driven by day-to-day decisions.'

▶ 'I would have more courage in taking risks in my career and relationships.'

▶ 'I would leave a legacy and have done more things for other people.'

The greatest regrets for people in their eighties were that they had not focused on identifying what their most important values were, and then set out to fulfil them.

Remember this

Regret for the things we have done can be tempered by time; it is regret for the things we have *not* done that is irreparable.

Metaphors in mind

TUNING INTO HOW OTHERS EXPERIENCE THE WORLD

No two people see the world in exactly the same way, but if you listen to the words they use you can begin to build up a picture of how they are experiencing the world. When you know what people are seeing and saying to themselves you can communicate with them more fully and join them in their worlds.

Have you ever wondered why people who witness the same event can have completely different interpretations of what happened? It is because they are seeing the world through their own filters. People tend to see whatever they are looking for. Whether this is hurts and slights from other people or love and acceptance, they will get what they look for and expect to happen.

Key idea: Metaphors paint pictures

A metaphor is a figure of speech that makes a point by stating something is like something else, when it is not literally true: 'He had nerves of steel', 'It was like wading through treacle', 'She was slippery as an eel'. Metaphors work by transferring observations or attributes from one set of circumstances to another.

The language we remember, that sticks in our minds, often employs metaphors rather than strict logic. Metaphors tend to be vivid and larger than life, descriptions that create a mental picture. If you listen to the people around you, you can learn a lot about the way they view the world simply by listening to the metaphors they use.

Wendy Sullivan of the Clean Change Company describes her image thus:

> 'Life is exciting. I see life as like a conveyor belt moving very fast with lots of presents wrapped up and coming past me. And I have to reach out and rip the paper off each present as quickly as possible so I can see what's inside. Otherwise my presents may get away.'

We may not know anything about Wendy but with a few deft visual brush strokes she has given us a picture and an insight into her world.

Here's the thing about metaphors or sayings that people use: when they liken one situation to another (i.e. 'Life is like a bowl of cherries'), they are describing how they are seeing the world at this particular time. The 'cherry' could mean that the person views the happenings in their world as ripe, juicy and ready to eat or explore. The words can mean different things to different people, but as soon as someone utters them we enter their world. We automatically imagine what we think the words mean to that person. We share their vision of the way they see the world. The more compelling the vision that someone sees, the more intensely they focus on drawing that outcome to themselves.

Try it now: Listening for other people's word pictures

Try out some other people's metaphors to see if it changes the way you see the world. If you are 'feeling stuck' in completing a task, try out a metaphor such as 'It's like surfing the waves' and note how it changes your view on the situation.

DO YOU HAVE A METAPHOR FOR LIFE?

What are the words you most often say to describe how life is for you now? 'Life is like a box of chocolates – you never know what you are gonna get,' as Forest Gump's mama said.

The images you play in your mind's eye and the words you repeat to yourself over and over again create your view of the world. Someone may say to you, 'Life is like a war zone,' which may mean to them that there is a lot of stress and they don't know what is going to happen next. Or 'Life is rosy,' which may mean life is particularly colourful and enhanced for that person at that time.

Some more examples might be:

▶ Life is like a roller-coaster – there are lots of ups and exciting bits and downs, which are the boring bits.

▶ Life is like an orchestra, where everyone is playing in tune.

▶ Life is like a seed – plant it and it will grow into a beautiful flower or a mighty tree.

- Life is like a great big canvas – I am excited; I want to throw all the paint I can at it.

- Life is like a deck of cards – you can't choose what you get, but you can decide how you play the game.

- Life is like a taxi – the meter's running whether you're going anywhere or not.

 Try it now: What is your metaphor or slogan for life?

1 What is the description you most consistently use about the way things are in life? Write it down:
- 'Life is like...'
2 On a scale of 1–10, how much control does your metaphor for life suggest you have over the outcomes in your life?
- A lot of control (scored 7–10)
- Some control (scored 4–6)
- Little or no control (0–3)
3 Are you happy with your metaphor for life and the effect it has on your outcomes?

Design a better metaphor for life

I watched some four-year-old children building a powerful metaphor for their own lives and actions based on a TV song called 'Bob the Builder'. When it came to the words 'Can he do it?' they all waved their arms in the air and shouted out, 'Yes he can!' They had stepped into Bob the Builder's world and become Bob. The children's body language changed – they were livelier – and they had developed a 'can do' attitude for the tasks ahead. They had set themselves up in a good learning state, one where they felt ready to tackle any new situation in a fun and energetic way. (This 'can do' metaphor also worked wonders for Barak Obama when he incorporated it into his 2008 presidential election slogan: 'Yes we can.') Can you see how using this powerful image gives the picture of a very capable person, building things, with all of his tools and resources attached to his workman's outfit?

It's time to design a better metaphor for your life, one that gives you more choices.

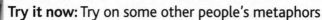

Try it now: Try on some other people's metaphors

1 If you could choose a better metaphor for life, one that aligns with the things you want to achieve, what would that metaphor be? Write it down:
   ▶ 'Life is like...'

2 What does (say being like Bob the Builder) your new metaphor for life let you think, believe or do that you could not do before?

3 Have you chosen a better metaphor for life, one that will see you succeeding more often in your goals?

4 What happens when you make the picture of your metaphor bigger, brighter, more colourful and closer, and you add sounds and emotions to accompany your image?

5 On a scale of 1–10, how much control does your metaphor for life suggest you have over the outcomes in your life?
   ▶ A lot of control (scored 7–10) – *Outstanding!*
   ▶ Some control, (scored 4–6) – *Gather your resources!*
   ▶ Little or no control (0–3) – *Major work ahead*

6 Have your scores increased from those for your previous, less motivating metaphor?

Try on other people's metaphors for life and find one that is pleasing to you – then make it your own. Having a fantastic and interesting metaphor to focus on gives you a stronger, more optimistic lens to view the world through and will open up lots of new possibilities.

Making sure your strategies work

Try it now: Test the evidence

Improved strategies will make your actions work for you, but test the evidence to be sure that this is the case. With any action you take, notice if changing your thinking, seeing or doing patterns of behaviour helps you make progress. Try the following method for testing your strategies:

1 Does my situation seem better or worse?
2 Describe in what way it has changed, and write the description down.
3 Can you see any new options that you could not see before?
4 How might you harness these new options and use them in your own situation?

Always look for evidence for whether what you are doing is working or not. Notice whether changing your metaphor for life has improved your willingness to see the world in a more optimistic light. What is your score on the 1–10 scale now? Do you feel more motivated about what lies ahead?

Focus points

By the end of this chapter you will have:

* Listed the tools and techniques you want to acquire
* Tuned into how others view the world, and the pictures that motivate them
* Learned how others use strategies to get the results they want
* Designed a better metaphor for life – one that gives you more choices.

Next step

In Chapter 2 we look at how you can adopt other people's successful strategies to maximize your own chances of achieving success.

2

Maximize the impact of whatever you do

In this chapter you will:

▶ *Explore strategies to maximize the impact of whatever you do*

▶ *Learn a successful strategy for doing it – now!*

▶ *Know how to anchor a confident state in stressful situations*

▶ *Try out a global thinking framework to help you think outside your box.*

One way of speeding up the process of getting more of the things you want from life is simply to notice how other people do things and notice what works for them. What we are doing by collecting their strategies is expanding the choices we have available to us. You can begin by listing some simple observable skills that are easy to acquire. What sort of skills could you use that would motivate you and enhance your beliefs about your abilities or advance your career and take you to the top? Start mining the attributes you see in the people around you, initially learning skills that are small, observable and easy to acquire. Choose skills that you need now, ones that will really help you towards achieving the things you want to do.

You don't need to reinvent the wheel – strategies are already out there for you to use. In what follows we will look at a few simple, but extremely powerful, examples:

▶ A strategy for using memory to recreate being in a good state

▶ A strategy for creating a good feeling

▶ A strategy for doing things now

▶ A strategy for being calm

▶ A strategy for thinking outside the box.

Be selective when choosing new strategies. You learn more easily when you are enthusiastic because you can identify how much leverage the new skill will give you in terms of what it will enable you to do that you cannot already do now. You learn more when you are genuinely curious to learn more, and continuously ask yourself the question: 'What will having this ability let me do that I cannot already do now?' In later chapters you will learn how to model a strategy yourself.

All skills and abilities are learnable, if you have the right resources. Maximize the impact of whatever you do by noticing the areas which you could improve in to increase your chances of succeeding. Notice the people who already have these skills, and list the ones you know will be most useful to you.

A strategy for using memory to recreate being in a good state

Your body retains the memories of past good or bad experiences you have had. With practice, you can access and enhance those memories and the accompanying feelings at will, and use them as a resource when you want to feel confident and successful in the future.

Try it now: Past memories are a powerful resource

Think back to one of the most wonderful days of your life. Remember that excited feeling, and feel it again. Relive a memory that pushes your hot button, a day when you achieved something that was memorable for you. You might have given a speech, passed an exam, hit a target, taken part in a sporting event, danced beautifully, did something fantastic that made you feel 'Wow! Whoosh! How did I really achieve that?' The impact that event has on you will be coloured by how vividly you imagine the scene.

There are ways of enhancing this technique. People who make dull, distant or disassociated pictures often feel disconnected from the event and lose their motivation. To increase the intensity of your 'feel good' feelings on your memorable day, you can rearrange your internal pictures so that you see things more intensely. To do this, try altering only one part of your memory at a time and see what happens. This way you can best gauge what type of images work best for you. There is part of your gathering of an evidence base so you know what does and what doesn't work for you.

Try it now: Set your mind to work for you

* Turn up the colour and brightness of your memory pictures, to see how your thoughts about the experience change. Did anything feel different when you did this?
* Make the event bigger and draw it closer to you, so that the scale, distance and intensity changes. What happens when you see things closer, and bigger, and brighter?
* Make sure you are 'associated' into the scene, and notice how things feel now. Are you experiencing the scene more intensely? Do you feel more motivated when you are actually in the scene?

Practise turning up the colour, increasing the scale and intensity of your goal, and see yourself in the scene to give it intensity. When you want confidence or to take more positive actions, then enhance your images, feel yourself being in the centre of your heart's desire. Feel yourself being in that strong 'Bob the Builder' confident state.

Try it now: Using your 'feel good' memory for the future

Think of situations in the future when you might need more confidence and a 'can do' attitude, a time when accessing your 'feel good' memory and sensations might stand you in good stead. Practise running an internal movie of your successful moments often, so that you can activate your feel good state at will. When you gather any new good sensations, anchor them, rehearse them and keep them with your other good sensation memories.

A strategy for creating a good feeling

People may say that they want wealth, power, control, supreme fitness, to drive a powerful expensive car… but at the end of the day it is what the experience *feels* like that will hook them into becoming motivated to have these things and not necessarily what it *looks* like. The following simple strategy will help you experience what achieving your goals might feel like.

Try this: Feeling good

Choose an experience that excites you and feel the intensity again. Imagine yourself as already having achieved your goals. See yourself sitting in the back seat of a luxury car, then feel the soft expensive leather. Smell the clean smell of polish, experience all the trappings that spell luxury to you. What are the things you are saying to yourself as you run through your mental movie? Pinpoint where in your body you first sense your molecules are beginning to dance with pleasure. Notice at what point the flush of excitement wells up inside you and spreads through your body. Take a mental snapshot of that moment of exhilaration so you can use it as a resource whenever you need to recall a good feeling.

A strategy for doing things now

Procrastination is the art of keeping up with yesterday. Procrastination is the result of unhelpful thinking habits that stop many people from achieving their goals. A common phrase is 'I meant to do it, but never got around to it!' People who procrastinate spend a lot of time beating themselves up and tend not to pay much attention to the outcome they want to achieve. They may spend their energy cycling through the emotions of anxiety, frustration, fear and threat.

If you are a person who procrastinates, then this chapter contains a very powerful gift. It provides a strategy for doing it now! Of course, you may be a compulsive completer and have to finish every task before you sleep, in which case a completion technique for procrastinators may be of no value to you. Throughout this book you need to choose and model the strategies that suit your needs.

From running training sessions, I have gathered almost a decade's worth of 'Do It Now!' strategies. Learners first discuss what their strategy for doing a task is and, if they have a tendency to procrastinate, notice at what point their technique begins to disintegrate. Then we ask the rest of the group, which usually contains a compulsive finisher, to explain their thinking patterns and beliefs around how they tackle a similar type of mission. This gives everyone a chance to try out different methods for becoming motivated and feeling compelled to complete tasks quickly.

If you are already happy with your 'Do It Now!' strategy – that's good. If not, you may want to elicit other people's strategies for achieving their successful outcomes.

Try it now: How do *you* become motivated to get things done?

Think back to the last three things you did when you had to mobilize your inner resources and take action in order for something to happen. It might have been when you changed your job, fixed something that was broken, passed a test or exam, or gave a presentation.

Did you wait until you could stand the situation no longer and felt forced to move on? (In which case you moved *away from pain*.) Or did you see something better, a new model with better prospects and jump at the chance of a new situation. (If you changed your situation from A to B in this way, you moved *towards pleasure*.)

Some people are motivated to get things done by moving away from pain – they envisage the pitfalls and what could go wrong. Some people are motivated to get things done by imagining the task as already completed.

Mark where you would put yourself on the 'Away from... – Towards...' continuum below:

Away from pain ◄─────────────────────────► *Towards pleasure*

Case study: Aviola – a compulsive finisher's 'Do It Now!' strategy

Aviola is a 'big picture' thinker and makes decisions and acts on them quickly. Once she gets motivated to do a task, she has a picture of the completed task and this spurs her on to finish the job.

Aviola first visualizes herself as already having completed the task, and asks:

1 **What are my steps?** She visualizes the first step and the outcome as already having occurred. She asks herself, 'What is the order I need to take my steps in?' and writes down a list of the things she needs to do to achieve her outcome.
2 **How do I do it?** She says: 'Being able to see the finished project in my mind, I can then work backwards to see how I did it and make a plan, do a drawing, or make a list so I know what to do. It is important I make a list, so I can tick things off as I do them. There is an immense satisfaction that comes from ticking things off.'
3 **How long will it take?** 'I break the task down into segments, so I know how long each bit takes. This lets me know how much I can expect to do each day.'

So, Aviola's steps are:

1 She visualises the task as already completed.

2 She visualizes the first step and then goes and does it. She ticks it off on her list.

3 She repeats this cycle until she has gone through all the steps.

By learning the beliefs, procedures and behaviours of a 'finisher', the 'procrastinator' can then try out the 'finisher's' strategy and notice whether it works for them. If the new method is helpful, they can then install the 'Do It Now!' strategy in their neurology and make it their own. If they stick with this method, and install it by using it over several projects, it will eventually become a habit that is part of their behaviour.

A strategy for remaining calm

Would it be useful to be able to remain calm during interviews, when taking tests, getting your point across in groups, giving talks or undergoing a stressful medical procedure? Then the following strategy which links confidence building to the visualization techniques we have already looked at might be helpful to you. A study carried out in England looking into ways to avoid the need to give general anaesthetics to claustrophobic patients attending for MRI scans recommended a similar anxiety-reducing technique. After learning the procedure, 76 per cent of patients underwent scans without GA. The results were advantageous in terms of both patient safety and costs.

The technique is rooted in a method for 'anchoring' good feelings.

We anchor memories throughout our lives. When we hear a few bars of familiar music and we want to jump up and dance, this indicates that we have anchored a behavioural response to a sensory stimulus. You may imagine a baby sleeping, its smile, its smell and warmth, and feel protective and loving. An anchor is any stimulus that changes your state.

Try it now: How to anchor a good feeling

1 Think about the situation that you are feeling anxious or nervous about. We want to replace the feeling with a more resourceful state.

2 List three or four more resourceful things you would need to feel to deal with the situation more positively. Breathe deeply and think of a time in the past when you already felt confident and deeply relaxed because you already had some calming resources.

3 See what you saw, hear what you heard, notice what you noticed and feel what you felt.

4 At the height of the experience when you are feeling really relaxed, anchor that good feeling with a small hand gesture you can easily repeat. Practise running and building your confident images. Make the feeling stronger, and stronger again. At the peak of each good experience, anchor the good feeling with a small hand gesture.

5 Now briefly think of having your unwanted procedure or whatever situation you are facing, then move out of it quickly. Go back to your really good feelings, press your fingers together to anchor that positive state, then step back into the negative spot bringing associations of all your good feelings with you.

6 Continue to associate into your positive anchors and build them so that you feel relaxed and happy, the way you want to feel in the future. Practise the anchoring sequence so that you are able to access your relaxed feelings on demand.

Remember this

As with any strategy, if you already know how to do it, or don't have any need for it, then it can seem useless. However, on the day it becomes pressing that you acquire a better way of handling a situation it becomes the most important ability that you can possess – because it gives you power and puts you in control of events.

A strategy for thinking outside the box

Knowing how someone who thinks completely differently from you sees the world gives you a vast array of new information. Any resulting changes in your behaviour, strategy or emotions transforms your beliefs and creates a cascade of new and different effects in your experience of what you can achieve in the world.

One major difference in thinking styles is that between the 'small detail' and 'big picture' thinker:

▶ **'Small detail', or procedural, thinker** Some people see situations up close and mainly from their own point of view. They tend to be procedural thinkers who ask themselves, 'Where do I fit in?' They may not be used to chunking up their thinking to take an overview of a situation in its entirety.

▶ **'Big picture', or global, thinker** Someone who is a global thinker is able to stand back and view situations from many different viewpoints and get the 'big picture'. He or she takes a global view of an idea or situation.

We have all met people who 'can't see the wood for the trees' or who, on the other hand, are so busy 'taking the global view' and 'seeing the big picture' that they don't pay attention to the detail of what is happening. These are extremes that illustrate how each of us tends to have a bias towards one style of thinking.

If you tend to be really good at remembering and handling detail, but lack an overall framework to relate it to, you probably do a lot of small chunk processing. If you are great at vision and planning, but get impatient with the details necessary to make your grand plan work, or overlook things that don't quite fit into the overall scheme, then you probably do a lot of large chunk processing.

If you want more information on how to tackle a situation from a different viewpoint, then notice who is getting good results, and notice how they do it. (If possible, use five or six different people who are getting good results so you can note the similar and different patterns in their thinking styles.) Which type of thinking would help you move on? Your aim is to become more flexible in your thinking and be able to chunk information up and down at will so that you can see a situation from every angle. For instance, having a few frames from a global thinking style can give you a working blueprint for gathering more insight into situations and coming up with more original and creative ideas.

In the following strategy, I show you how you might use 'big picture' thinking to expand your creative options. This is a fun exercise that I often use at the beginning of a training session. Using a global thinker's thought patterns sparks new insights and moves people on in their thinking around a situation. By the end of the day users find their thinking has shifted and moved forward.

Try it now: Thinking outside of the box

1 Choose a situation for which you would like to gain a solution, or into which you would like more insight. The situation might be...

✻ **your own:** you might want to change direction, do something different, but not know how best to proceed

✻ **your community's:** your local authority may want to close a library, a hospital, a valuable service — you need a plan for how you might rally and develop alternative solutions.

2 Write down your situation and your current thinking about it in a sentence or two, so that you have evidence for whether your thinking has moved on or not after the thinking-through session is done.

3 Now apply the following questions to your situation. Ask the questions out loud, and wait for the answers to come to you.

✻ **Question 1**   What am I seeing that others are missing in this situation? (e.g. Do behaviour and outcome not add up?)

✻ **Question 2**   What are the things I am noticing? Is it that people's focus is on the wrong thing? Is attention focused on the biggest problem or something small? What are the things that are acting as a distraction to thinking?

✻ **Question 3**   What has been happening to hamper finding a good-fit solution before now? Is this rational or emotive behaviour I am witnessing (from myself/from others)? How might people's behaviour affect the outcome?'

✻ **Question 4**   What is the scope for change? What are the options? How can I make a difference? How much energy do I have to do this task?

4 After completing this exercise, answer the following:

✻ Do you have a different perspective on the situation?

✻ Have your ideas moved on?

✻ Do you have a solution, or the start of another idea, in mind?

✻ Write down how your ideas have shifted.

Once you crack the code to recognizing other people's thought processes, you have a simple tool you can use in any circumstances throughout your lifetime. The process requires that you look and listen for what these people focus on in a situation. Start to notice how they are seeing the world, and what they are saying to themselves about events. You are noticing how other people filter incoming information they get from the outside world.

Focus points

By the end of this chapter you will:

✳ Have gained an overview of what you can achieve by using other people's strategies

✳ Have acquired some useful 'software' strategies for the brain that can move you closer to achieving your aims

✳ Know how to anchor a confident state in stressful situations

✳ Have used a global thinking framework to help you think outside of your box.

Next step

By this point you will have achieved some clarity on what you want to do, what it will look like to do it, and have generated some options for how you might achieve your outcomes. But remember, your actions need to be set within a larger goal-setting framework – and this is the subject covered in Chapter 3.

3

Set and achieve any goal you choose

In this chapter you will:

- ► *Learn how to develop a goal-setting plan*
- ► *Install and practise the six principles for goal-achieving success*
- ► *Discover how to gain leverage from every goal you set*
- ► *Identify your motivation and commitment for setting your goals*
- ► *Set a new goal – and take steps towards achieving it.*

Hope is not a good goal-setting strategy

> 'Having hope and faith are essential, but something more
> is needed; the skill and discipline to organize your brain in
> ways that will successfully motivate your life.'
>
> Mark Robert Waldman, American neuroscientist and therapist

Many people use words like 'hope', 'wish', 'would like' when
planning outcomes. However, by using these words you are
implying that what you want is something that is outside of
your own capability or control. You need to be sure that your
goals are stated in such a way as to seem probable, not just
possible: for instance 'I will get fit enough to run a marathon',
not 'I wish I was fit enough' or 'I would like to be fit enough' or
'I hope I will be fit enough.'

When you know how to maintain your level of motivation, how
you set your goals, and how to follow through with positive
actions, you hold the key to success in every area of your life.
The art of conscious goal setting is one of the most invaluable
mental tools you will ever possess.

> 'Make decisions. Live your life through decisions rather
> than habits. You will have more control over your life, and
> enjoy greater success.'
>
> Peter Thomson, UK business strategist

Successful goal-achieving strategies are not just useful for
business purposes. They link in to every other area of your life,
be it financial, career, social, family, mental, physical or spiritual.
How we picture ourselves, whether it's as a success or failure,
ultimately affects our level of confidence and self-esteem and our
beliefs about the things we are capable of achieving in the future.

> 'Planning without action is futile.
> Action without planning is fatal.'
>
> Goal-setting maxim

Your habits are what drive your goals; they determine whether
you get what you want or you don't. The habits you have got
right now are based on being motivated enough to achieve
whatever you have gained to date. So, if you want to achieve
more, you will have to break habits that are designed for getting

you whatever you are getting now. Whatever your goals have been to date, you need to think bigger.

Choose goals that when you achieve them will make a big difference to your life. If you are feeling a bit of doubt, uneasiness and puzzlement, that is good. If you are feeling comfortable and relaxed, then your goal setting is not working – you are simply doing more of the same. To make sure you that become a goal achiever, instead of just a goal setter – think big, and take actions to ensure that you are stepping outside of your comfort zone.

We have already looked at some really powerful tools: using visualization and other people's success strategies can give you massive leverage when setting your goals. It is a good idea to spend ten minutes running through a visualization, focusing and goal-setting process every day.

Try it now: Choose goals that have consequences

Take a look at your life and ambitions to date and begin to define your goals. List the headings under which you want to achieve them, for example:

* Business
* Work
* Money
* Health
* Relationships

Under each heading, write a list of things you would like to achieve, then clearly define each goal and how you will achieve it. Include a description that covers how you would like things to change. Do not worry about how you are going to achieve your goal at present.

Start with a general statement, such as:

* 'I want to increase my earnings.'
* 'I want to run my own business.'
* 'I want to run a marathon.'
* 'I want to write a bestseller.'

Now refine your list and make your ingredients more detailed. If you have said that you want to increase your earnings, then get down to the specifics: write down by how much and over what period of time this will happen and write down a target date. Then brainstorm as many ways as possible in which you could make it happen.

Develop a goal-setting plan

Strategies are plans for getting things done. You are more likely to reach your goals when they become steps in an overall strategy. Your chances of succeeding at whatever you want to do get better when you:

▶ know what you want and in what context you want to excel in

▶ have a route map for getting there

▶ set recognizable markers along the way that will let you know that you are on target

▶ have a process in place for getting you there.

Stack all your goals in the same direction, so that they flow together towards your ultimate aims (remember that quote about 'Lining your ducks up in a row'!). That means clarifying your goals so that you know exactly what you want and in what circumstances, and eliminating any negative beliefs you may hold about your capabilities that may otherwise hold you back.

Visualize reaching your goals and run lots of action replays, so that you taste and see and experience the emotions of what your achievements will look like when you hold them in the palm of your hand.

Break your goals down into different component parts. This will make goals easier to achieve. If you learn how to operate the six following principles, you can ensure that your outcomes are focused and rewarding. These are the foundation principles of success upon which neuro-linguistic programming is based. If you take away nothing else from this book except this model, you will have still increased your ability to achieve the things you want to in life.

The Principles for Success are:

1 Begin with your end in mind.

2 Use your senses to notice what is happening.

3 Be flexible - if what you are doing is not working, then try something else.

4 Build and maintain good relationships ('rapport').

5 Operate from a confident state.

6 Take action! – without action nothing can be achieved.

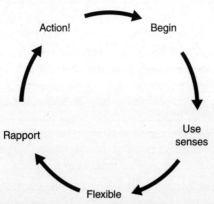

Figure 3.1 The Principles for Success – use this model as a framework for every new goal you set. This is a way of ensuring that the Principles for Success become installed in your neurology.

The Principles for Success

Let's look at each of these in a bit more detail:

1 **Begin with your end in mind.** Never start a project without having worked out what the result is that you want is in advance, particularly if the outcome is important to you.

2 **Use your senses to notice what is happening.** Notice what is going on around you. What do you notice about the other people involved in the situation. How do you feel about the situation. What are the gut feelings in your body telling you? Write down or vocalize what your body is telling you out loud.

3 **Be flexible.** If what you are doing is not working, then try something else. How often do you see people repeat the same behaviour over and over again, hoping for a different result? Some people repeat the same sorts of working or relationship patterns again and again, even though it fails to get them the outcome they want. If it is a pattern of behaviour you are locked into and it's not working – then change it for something else. Anything else that will get a different result.

4 **Build and maintain good relationships ('rapport').** Build good
   relationships with yourself and other people. That means
   creating win-win situations with the people around you, and
   also being good to yourself. Often, that means challenging
   the gremlins in our heads that tell us negative things about
   ourselves and undermine our potential performance.

5 **Operate from a confident state.** When you begin a project, clearly
   define what it is you want to achieve. Use your senses to notice
   what is happening, and take appropriate action to change anything
   that is not working. When you become flexible and able to change
   your behaviour to get the outcomes you want, and build good
   relationships with yourself and others, then change happens. Your
   confidence is built on installing the principles for success in your
   muscles, so that it becomes a natural way to behave.

6 **Take action!** Without action nothing else happens. There are
   people who seem extremely knowledgeable, have great ideas, they
   talk about a goal, busy themselves with it, yet for some reason
   nothing comes to fruition. That is because their idea stops short
   at the thinking stage – they never take action. An idea is only a
   notion – for it to become reality, an action has to happen.

Try it now: Installing the Principles for Success

List some immediate goals that you want to achieve. They should be
outcomes that excite you, even compel you to do them. Ensure that the
goals you set are hard enough to move you out of your comfort zone, but
not so difficult that failure would absolutely crush you. Then write these
questions down and then note your answers to them:

1 What are my immediate goals?
2 What are my mid-term goals?
3 What are the things that are really important to me?

You may have come up with career goals or wanting a different lifestyle, to
travel, or to build strong relationships. Is there something in life that makes
your heart sing because you really want to do it?

When you have written a list of goals ask these questions about each goal
you want to achieve:

1 What is important to me about having this goal?
2 Am I interested in meeting and achieving some worthwhile goals in my
   life? (You might be interested in becoming an athlete, a career professional,
   a creative person whose achievements live on after you are gone.)

If you are simply interested in these things, you will not commit. However, if you are doing this because you want to be the best at whatever you choose, you will make the decision to become committed, and then you will achieve whatever you want.

Try it now: Committing to your goals

Write down your answers to the following questions:

1 Why do you want this goal?
2 What does it let you do?

Once you have the *why*, the *what* follows:

1 What is important to you about having this goal?
2 What does having this goal say about you?
3 What are the associated words that come to mind? For example, 'Running my own business will give me "freedom", "challenge", "options", "excitement", "risks", "opportunities".'
4 What new insight have you gained about yourself and the things that are important to you? Will gaining one new goal gain you leverage and open up greater and more impactful benefits to you?

Remember this

People who are committed don't make excuses. They take responsibility for everything that is happening in their world. They don't blame other people, circumstances, lack of education or bad luck; they take responsibility for everything that happens in their world. If your thoughts are taken up with blaming 'circumstances', this causes lack of energy and lack of focus on your purpose.

Try it now: What would be your biggest regrets?

At the end of your life, what are the things you would most regret not having done to date? Make a list.

Of these things you have listed, how many of them might be possible for you now? If you were really serious above achieving one of these goals, what might be the very next action you could take today to achieve this outcome. It might be to make a phone call, gather some information, draw a plan, talk to someone who has already done it, read a book. Whatever you decide on, do it!

Case study: Gemma Bailey – using the Principles for Success

Gemma Bailey used the Principles for Success when undertaking what was eventually a successful career swap.

Gemma says: 'I wanted to change my career. However, I started out as a nursery nurse and had a very specific qualification in nursery nursing and some management skills. I also had the benefits of an NLP course I had attended as part of my training.

'My friend and fellow NLP trainer suggested doing something new and niche with our NLP skills which combined the skills we had. She suggested working specifically with children, which I initially thought was a bad idea, and came up with the idea for NLP4Kids. However, after promoting NLP4Kids on our website, we had three enquiries in the first three days. Then I realised it was a great idea!

'We did a workshop every month for three months and my private practice started going crazy with people bringing their children to see me. About a year in I had people coming from all over the country and knew that we should be sharing our skills with others who could be using them in their area of the world. That was when I decided we should license NLP4Kids to others. There are now people running NLP4Kids workshops in different parts of the world.'

How Gemma used the principles for success:
* She moved towards pleasure and what would make her happy.
* She knew her values, the things she considered to be important to her.
* She gathered her resources, listed the skills she already had and what she could put them towards.
* She already knew how she would feel when she had achieved her heart's desire.

Using Gemma's case study we can see how important the Six Principles were in achieving her goal.

1 **Start with your end in mind.** Gemma knew she wanted to change her career; she wanted freedom to do things she enjoyed and engage her creativity. It had to be something completely different from nursery nursing that enabled her to use her existing skills and then build on them. At this

point she may not have known exactly what she wanted but she knew how she wanted to *feel*. Her value words were 'freedom', 'enjoy' and 'creative'.

2 **Use your senses to notice what is happening.** Sensing how she wanted to feel, and knowing the skills she already possessed, Gemma's new opportunities and options began to appear. Gemma noticed a gap in the market – there were no courses around that provided children with practical solutions for overcoming emotional challenges, to increase their confidence and to build their self-esteem so that they could reach a greater learning potential.

3 **Be flexible** If what you are doing is not working, then try something else. Gemma answered the *hard* questions. (Many people don't stay with the hard questions long enough to reach a solution – because it makes them feel uncomfortable.) The difficult questions are the ones you need to stay with until options and solutions begin to appear, even when the process feels uncomfortable.

4 **Build and maintain good relationships ('rapport').** Gemma was aware that she had good rapport skills with people, with her working partner and, especially, with children.

5 **Operate from a confident state.** Gemma had a positive attitude about her abilities and an outcome to attach it to. (People who have a positive attitude, but no focus as to where to apply that attitude, tend to burn out!) Gemma had a strategy – that is, a plan for achieving her outcome.

6 **Take action!** Without action, nothing happens! She tested the water first by promoting NLP4Kids on her website, which generated some interest, then did one workshop a month for three months and her private practice built up. That was when she decided to license NLP4Kids to others: 'There are now people running workshops in different parts of the world.'

Try it now: Clarify your goals

Using Gemma's case study to prompt you, choose one of your own goals (the one that draws you the most) and apply each of the Principles of Success to it in turn.

When you have finished, write down each of the steps you will need to take in order to achieve your aim in life.

Remember this: Most people don't have a working plan

Ninety-four per cent of the population does not think strategically. Using the Six Principles framework will immediately put you ahead.

Setting SMART goals

Your goals are most likely to be achieved when they are set within a framework. The more aspects of the task you have thought about in advance, the more likely you are to succeed. This is a very simple goal-setting procedure you can quickly do in your head, provided you remember the mnemonic SMART and what the letters stand for. It is useful if you need to make an immediate decision and take an action quickly.

SPECIFIC	Goals are **specific** – they are actions you can take that lead in the direction of your purpose. Your goals should be personal to you, although they may link into someone else's goals.
MEASURABLE	Goals are **measurable**, which allows you to judge how much progress you have made towards reaching your target.
ACHIEVABLE	Goals should be **achievable** – not so easy that they don't tax you, not so hard that you regularly fail to reach them and so become disillusioned.
REALISTIC	Your goals should be **realistic** and fit in with who you are and what you are capable of. If you set yourself too rigorous goals, and then fail to achieve them, you are likely to become dejected. If your goals are too easy, you are unlikely to feel the elation that comes with real achievement.
TIMEFRAME	Goals should be set within a definite **timeframe**. They should also have definite markers along the route so that you can tell whether you are doing well or need to change some of your tactics.

Try it now: Set a SMART goal

Using the mnemonic SMART and checking back to remember what each letter stands for...

1 Take one of your own goals and run it through the SMART goal scenario to check if it meets the criteria for being a SMART goal.
2 Check that your goals is: **S**pecific, **M**easurable, **A**chievable, **R**ealistic and set within a **T**imeframe. (Many people fail at goal setting because they don't set a timescale in which to take the actions.)
3 Plan to launch the start of your goal within 24 hours.
4 Write down the action points and timings, that is: start date and time, and finishing date for completion of your task. Unless you have a completion date – your task is open-ended!

Set your goal in context

Our goals are not set in isolation; they are usually connected to each other and involve other people, things and situations. Constantly ask yourself, 'When I achieve this outcome, what else might it lead to? where else might it take me?'

Use the following list when planning your goals – it will help you think about the context of your plan, the possible ramifications of the decisions you make, and where it might lead you.

1 **Set your outcomes.** Think about something you really burn to achieve, something that is difficult enough to excite you, but not totally beyond your abilities. From your list of goals that you made near the beginning of this chapter, is there one that it is imperative for you to reach now, one that hinges to lots of other important aims in your life?

2 **Define your goals clearly.** What do you want? You may already have some definite goals in mind but, if you don't, pick something that is important to you in relation to your life's ambitions.

3 **Imagine that you have already achieved your outcome.** What are the things that you will see, hear, feel and experience that will let you know you have achieved your goal? Athletes practise this kind of technique every day, imagining they have hit the ball, run the race, or lifted the weight, living the

experience many times over before the actual event. In this way, they use all of their sensory apparatus to see things they might not otherwise see, play through and correct different actions in their imagination, and feel all the feelings associated with performing brilliantly and achieving success. When they walk on to a pitch, into a stadium, up to a pool table or into a boxing ring, they have success hard-wired into their neurology.

4 **Check for any side-effect you haven't thought of.** In what circumstances do you want this outcome? Is it work, home, social ...? Are there any circumstances in which you *wouldn't* want it? For instance, your aim might be to acquire better leadership skills so that you can take on a more challenging role in your work. But would you want to carry those skills over into your dealings with your friends or family? Be aware that your change in thinking style and behaviour in work, if carried into other areas of your life, might change the dynamics of your relationships.

5 **How will having this outcome affect the people around you?**– your business associates, work colleagues, partner, family, friends? Sometimes relationships break up because one partner is striving to be more successful while the other stays the same. If your goal will affect your whole family, involve them and get them to buy into what you are doing at an early stage.

6 **What will you gain from achieving this outcome?** What do you get from what you are presently doing? Will you lose anything you value by achieving your outcome? Some business entrepreneurs pay the price of losing their first marriage when they undertake a goal because their beliefs and values evolve while their partner's remain the same.

7 **Have you the control, resources and time you need?** How much control do you have over this outcome? You will probably never have complete control, but the more you can influence the outcome, the more likely you are to achieve it.

8 **What resources do you have?** What skills, understanding, information, time do you need to achieve this outcome? Do you have them already, or do you know how to get them? Do you need money? Often, when you think through a situation, you realize that you don't need money. You need what money will *buy* you – so barter.

9 **What is a realistic timeframe to achieve your goal within?** Most people work better under deadlines, and if you don't set deadlines then your work may expand to fill the spare time in which you have to do it. Telling others about your plan and announcing the completion date can give you extra motivation to complete if you start to waver.

10 **Obstacles** What will you do about anything that might get in the way? If you are dealing with other people or events, bottlenecks and delays are likely to occur. Write a list of what these might be and then detail several options you could take to get you past the hurdle. For example, if the delay involves another person agreeing to complete a task by a certain date and you think they won't meet your deadline, ask them at the beginning of the project, 'Can I have your word on that?'

11 **To what is this goal, and your actions, a bridge?** Achieving goals opens doors to other possibilities, so always be on the lookout for other opportunities.

12 **Look ahead.** What would having this outcome say about you as a person?

13 **If you achieve this outcome, what else will you get?** What is the next step to achieving this outcome?

Now ask yourself: 'Do I still want this outcome?'

Try it now: How to set and achieve any goal you choose

Choose something that is really important to you and will make a difference to your life. For example, you might want to work in a clutter-free environment, so that you don't waste time looking for papers, become stressed, or miss deadlines. Using the list above, work through your plan and consider any ramifications it may have and any problems you will meet along the way.

1 Set your outcome.

✱ *Goal 1:* 'I will [e.g. clear clutter form my desk] by [date].'

2 Define your goal.

... and so on.

Now ask yourself: 'Do I still want this outcome?'

Remember this: Set goals in a context

Goals that are set in relation to others are more likely to be completed, even when the going gets tough, whereas ones set in isolation are more likely to be abandoned if things don't go to plan.

Tips for setting goals

▶ **Break down your goals into small bite-sized chunks.** A complete project, such as breaking into and saturating a sales market, or being slim, supple and active, or earning a million pounds, may seem daunting. So break down your steps into chunks and be determined each day to take some small steps towards achieving your goal.

▶ **Focus on the progress you are making each day.** To write this book and fit it into an already full time schedule, I kept a time-log diary with a page for each day that I worked on the project. From this I learned what was working and what wasn't.

▶ **Think about your goal constantly.** See yourself achieving your goal and run action movies in your mind. Use all your senses of seeing, hearing, feeling, taste and smell to associate with your picture more fully. See your movie from different angles, so that, if there are obstacles, you can view the problem from another perspective.

▶ **Commit your goals to writing.** Keep your goals simple and use concrete words. 'I want to be thinner' is not a goal; it is a wish. 'I want to be two kilos thinner in three weeks' gives you a timeframe and target. Write down, too, the specific markers you will see, hear and feel that will let you know that you have reached your aim – for example, 'I will feel fitter and look fabulous in a new outfit.'

▶ **Goals should be time specific.** You may have an overall goal, say, over ten years. Break it down into yearly segments and have monthly check-ups to assess how you are doing. Have regular weekly planning sessions, say on Friday afternoons, where you build your lists for the following week and work on daily improvements.

▶ **Dealing with obstacles.** When you encounter obstacles to your goals, imagine how people who have already achieved a similar outcome would do it. Take three of these successful people and ask yourself how they would approach this task. Take your time and wait for the answers to come.

▶ **Work smarter – not harder.** Often, it's necessary to work extremely hard to get a project started. But if this means that you are constantly working under pressure, working long hours or not getting enough sleep, your standard of work and ability to think strategically will suffer. Don't get so tied up in your project that you don't have time for anything else. You know where you're heading, so be good to yourself along the way. Take some time to smell the roses, and give yourself some enjoyment and lots of little rewards.

▶ **Catch yourself doing things well.** Keep a daily events diary of your progress, listing your highs and lows. Look especially for clues to see what triggered changes in your motivation levels, especially the changes that took you from 'Can't do' to 'Yes, I'm doing it'. When you know how these states were created you can create them intentionally.

▶ **Do a 'look-back' exercise.** At the end of every project you undertake, do a 'look-back' exercise – review and write down what worked well for you and what didn't work. Look at ways of getting better and of improving your efficiency. Keep your feedback notes handy, so they are available to you next time you start on a similar goal. That way you can build up and store your criteria for achieving a fantastic outcome in the future.

▶ **Review your goals regularly.** Besides asking 'Am I on target?', also ask yourself: 'Do I still want this outcome?' Are you still whole-heartedly committed to the initial goals you set yourself, or have new possibilities arisen that might take you on another course. People who don't review their goals regularly can end up reaching their target and then finding out it wasn't what they wanted after all.

▶ **Get into the habit of setting goals and achieving them.** Start first with small goals and practise going for them with the same level of determination you will carry through to your larger projects. Start by aiming for easy goals so that you can hone your techniques and see yourself as a winner. The more frequently you experience success, the easier it is to expect that you will get the things you want from life and the more likely you are to get them.

Try it now: How to become a goal achiever – 21 days to successful goal achievement

If you intend to change events in the outside world, then a good way to check that your goal-setting techniques are working well is to set yourself an 'inner-space' goals on a personal level – one that involves either changing a habit, for example slimming, getting fit, giving up something, or learning to do something new.

Your motivation level is likely to drop when you set goals over a long period of time ('I want to be thin in six months' time – but this chocolate bar is beside me right now' or 'I want to run a mini-marathon, but I can't seem to get out of bed right now'). A lot of your initial enthusiasm that bubbled up when you hatched your plan may disappear if you think so far ahead. For a lot of people, 21 days is the length of time it takes to install a new habit, so plan your goal in clearly defined chunks to be achieved over three weeks.

* **Select a goal to work on for 21 days.** It must be something that you really want to achieve and are prepared to give your attention to for this length of time.
* **Take one chunk of your goal that you know can be accomplished in three weeks' time.** For example, if your goal is to lose two kilos in 21 days, then break it down into daily tasks. Initially, you might read some advice on nutrition, and work out where and at what times of day your trigger points for eating chocolate cake kick in. Over the first few days you might decide you will spend an extra 20 minutes each morning planning your day ahead and preparing your own lunches, so you are less likely to go off course.
* **Look back over the previous days to see what worked and what didn't.** For example, you might now decide how to plan your evening meals when you are satisfied your new habit has been installed.
* **Avoid 'all or nothing' thinking.** If you encounter obstacles – say your goal is slimming and one day you eat chocolate cake – don't assume that, because you didn't achieve that day's target, your whole project

is a failure; it isn't so. Be kind to yourself and allow for two 'relaxation days' when you can relax your new habit.

* **If you are not an avid plan setter**, then draw large red dots on your calendar beside each allotted day. Write what you hope to achieve at the beginning, and on target days write in what you hope to have achieved by that day.

* **Plan your rewards.** In our slimming example, you could treat yourself at the end of every five-day period, or whenever you are likely to go astray if you are not pampered in some way. Seeing your goal written on your calendar in advance will keep you on course. If you promise yourself something special for staying on target, then do it; otherwise you might have a relapse.

Once you have achieved your 21-day systematic approach to goal setting, check over the next few days to ensure that your new habit is installed and has become part of your thinking habit and part of your regular routine.

Focus points

By the end of this chapter you will have:

✳ Learned how to develop a goal-setting plan
✳ Practised and installed the six principles for achieving successful goals
✳ Summarized how you will develop a goal-setting plan
✳ Identified your motivation for, and commitment to, setting your goals
✳ Set a new goal – and taken steps towards achieving it!

Next step

Our values drive us and are what brings meaning to our lives. Knowing which values are uppermost in your mind is the key to you leading a rewarding life. When we set our goals in alignment with our values, we are in a situation where we create flow. The next chapter is about discovering your values and motivation.

Align your values and motivation

In this chapter you will:

▶ *Learn how values drive us and provide meaning in our lives*

▶ *Identify your own values*

▶ *Discover how knowing your values increases motivation and peak performance*

▶ *Find out more about the power of positive images and anchoring.*

When did you last check your values?

Key idea

Motivation begins with bringing our values to the things that we do.

How often do you see people engaging in escapist behaviour? Disconnected from their values, they spend their time on automatic pilot. They may aimlessly pass time on computer sites or flip TV channels for hours on end, hoping to find something to amuse or hold their attention briefly. When we become disconnected from our values, we lose motivation and no longer feel we have a purpose in life.

To be motivated by your values, you first need to be given the tools that enable you to understand what your own values are and how you can align them with the values of the people you connect with. Knowing about values helps build relationships with others in ways that bring more meaning to everyone's lives.

Try it now: Reflect on what motivates you

Think back to a time when you were really motivated to get things done:

* What type of tasks did you want to complete?
* Were they simple things like getting out of bed, or getting to an appointment? Or were they more complicated outcomes where the payoff was greater?
* Note whether your motivation for doing the same task ever changes.
* If your motivation for doing the same thing does change, what are the circumstances this is dependent on?

Start thinking about the things you value most. Use the following list to prompt you and add your own values to it:

achievement	ethics	honour
adventure	family	health
beauty	freedom	honesty
charity	friendship	humility
community	fun	independence
creativity	growth	individuality
dignity	happiness	integrity

intimacy	pride	spirituality
justice	reason	strength
kindness	respect	supportiveness
knowledge	risk	trust
leadership	security	truth
love	self-discipline	wisdom
peace	self-esteem	
power	service	

Pick ten values that are most important to you. Beside each one write the reason why this value is important to you. You might write:

creativity Creativity is important to me because... it lets me express myself.

freedom Freedom is important to me because... I want the freedom to decide what I do.

The purpose is to get a sense of whether your motivation for having each value is directed to getting more of what you want (moving towards your goal), or to getting away from what you do not want (moving away from discomfort).

Now rank your list of values in order of priority from 1 to 10.

If you cannot decide whether you rate one quality over another, write the individual words on pieces of paper and put them face upwards on the palms of each hand. Look at the words on each piece of paper in turn and balance them as if you were using weighing scales until an outright winner emerges. Repeat the procedure with all the pieces of paper until you have your values rated in order of priority.

Now ask yourself, 'What do I value most in life?'

Remember this
There is a scene at the beginning of the film *City of Angels* where a little girl lies ill in a hospital bed. Moments later we see her walking slowly down the corridor holding the hand of an angel. The angel turns to her and asks, 'What was the best bit for you? What did you really enjoy about being alive?'

Having a deep awareness of your values is inspiring, motivating and enlightening. Regularly explore your values and discover what means most to you in your life. To experience your values in a heartfelt way, ask yourself some questions so that you can begin to connect your values with actual needs, objectives and actions you can take.

Try it now: Explore your values

Chunk your values down by asking these questions:

* What are the things I am most grateful for having in my life?
* What are the specific actions I can take to bring more of these things into my life?
* What do I really value about the work I do?
* What abilities do I bring to this area of my life?
* What is important to me about my relationships?
* Am I happy about the way I relate to others?
* What capabilities could I acquire that would help me to relate to others even better?

Write your answers down so that you can go back, reflect on them, and update them.

Key idea

Motivation is strongest when you move towards what gives you energy, and away from what depletes your energy.

Reflect on each area of your life regularly, and ask:

▶ What can I do today that excites me and gives me energy?

▶ What can I do today that aligns with my beliefs and values?

▶ What can I do today that fuels my passions and takes me in the direction of my purpose in life?

Follow your values to increase motivation

Motivation and peak performance come from knowing what you want to achieve in life. Many of us move through life with a few goals and objectives but without a real sense of purpose. Our goals are often more about what we *don't* want rather than moving towards the things we *do* want. We might say we want a better job, partner or home, but our main wish is to get away from our current situation.

Here are some positive assumptions to adopt for achieving peak performance:

Positive assumption	Reason
If what you are doing is not working, do something else.	If you do what you have always done, you will get what you have always got.
There is no failure, only feedback. What really matters is that you learn from the results.	Whatever occurs, you can use the feedback to change your future behaviour and improve your results.
People have all the resources they need to make changes that will make a difference to their performance.	There is always something you can do to make a difference and the answer is usually an inner resource.
We all have different versions and viewpoints about how we view reality. To build rapport with someone, join them in their world.	We filter information about the world through our senses and each person focuses on different aspects and creates different models of reality.
You cannot change another person; you can only change yourself.	Changing your behaviour will change other people's responses to you.
Visualizing and thinking about the changes you want to make are the first step to making improvements in your life.	Changes start off as thoughts; they are structured and communicated in pictures and words and becomes actions.

Be happy now

A popular belief is that we must have 'things' to make us happy. When contemplating future goals many people imagine that their goal must happen before they can start to really live. We put conditions on our happiness because we believe that getting the things we want is dependent on other people and events which are outside our control.

We begin the cycle of deferred happiness by thinking 'I will be happy when…':

▶ 'I will be happy when I meet the right person.'

▶ 'I will be happy when I get the job I want.'

▶ 'I will be happy when I get the right car, television, house.'

▶ 'I will be happy when I am immensely rich and successful.'

Remember this

Think of happiness as being what happens when you consciously notice and enjoy experiencing pleasure, then use your energy and motivation to connect to your values and the sensations that you can enjoy that give you pleasure. Make a list of the many things that bring you happiness. It can be anything from a thrilling sport which invigorates you to early-morning meditations, connecting to other people, stroking your pet ... that first cup of tea in the morning!

Try it now: Feel good *before* you achieve your outcome

1 Think about a particular goal you want to achieve. It might be 'I want to become the best person that anyone could choose to hire in my particular area of expertise.'

2 Now imagine that you already are that person: feel it, see it, hear it. Answer the following questions:
   ▶ What are the extra qualities you, as your successful future self, possess that may not have been present before?
   ▶ What extra skills have you acquired, and why?

3 Write down three new beliefs you are holding about your future self and your abilities that make you feel happy and assured of your future success. Start with a simple statement, for example:
   ▶ 'Clients/jobs/partners/breaks in life [whatever it is for you] are easy to come by because I have these beliefs or qualities...'

4 Tell yourself that it is true, and then listen to your inner voice and gather evidence to support your belief. For example, 'I know that I am a fabulous therapist, the best that anyone could possibly have because...' Then listen and gather information from your subconscious about the sort of behaviour, capabilities and beliefs that you would need to support what you have said.

POSITIVE IMAGES

The images we repeatedly run in our mind's eye, and the words we constantly repeat to ourselves, create our mental maps of the world.

If we have a 'scarcity mentality', then we dwell on images of what is *lacking* in our lives. We invest our mental energy into what we don't have, and our experience of life is 'I don't have enough love/money/time/energy, etc.', because our mind is caught up in what is missing.

People who see positive images in their mind will look for and expect good things to happen and notice and remark on it when it does. Their mind is caught up with what is positive and abundant in their lives.

Our actions come from the pictures we constantly run in our minds. Many people believe that they do not have control over what images they see, or the thoughts that they think, and thus they are not in control of their lives. But we can change our perceptions of the world by changing the way we choose to view it, and once we do this we can begin to create our future circumstances.

Mental rehearsal prepares you for events and trains your unconscious mind to perform tasks in a predetermined way. Most physical tasks, such as breathing, walking, driving a car, are carried out unconsciously, once the initial preparation work of learning has been done. By mentally rehearsing future successful outcomes you are communicating with your mind through pictures, inner dialogue, feelings, tastes and smells, and building up patterns about how events will play out.

USE ANCHORS TO CHANGE YOUR STATE OF MIND
We looked at anchoring in Chapter 2, but as it is a key skill to practise I return to it again here.

We anchor memories throughout our lives. An anchor is any stimulus that changes your state. A smell of a particular soap or perfume may evoke strong memories of people or places you have known and loved. An anchor is a stimulus that leads to a response. You can use anchoring when you feel nervous, shy or anxious or when you are experiencing negative feelings; at such times you can choose to anchor a positive state instead.

To anchor a feeling, say of confidence, think back to a past experience when you did something really well. You felt confident, and motivated and powerful, the way you would like to feel in the future.

You can use anchors to put yourself in a good state before an interview, presentation or exam, in fact any situation where you need to feel confident and good about yourself. By thinking of a time when you were at your best, it will make you feel more confident and ready to handle the next challenge you meet. Think about what makes you feel successful and in a really confident state.

Try it now: Anchor a confident state

1 Think of a time when you did something really well and felt completely confident.
2 Go back in time and step into your body, see what you see, feel what you feel, hear what you hear.
3 Close your eyes and relive that experience. What were you seeing, hearing, feeling?
4 At the peak of the experience anchor that state with a small movement or gesture you can replicate with ease. (Try pressing your thumb and middle finger together at the height of the feeling, so that when you repeat the gesture the good feeling repeats itself again.)
5 Recall that good feeling often, so that you carry it with you wherever you go. Use it as a personal resource.
6 Practise the sequence five or six times so that you are able to access the confident feeling on demand.

Key idea

Neuroscientists have identified that when we have pleasant rewarding experiences it triggers the amygdala in our brain to register the emotional intensity of an experience and releases dopamine in our brain. Dopamine is what produces the 'feel good' factor. Dopamine is a substance we crave because it makes us feel good about ourselves.

Anchoring good feelings has been around a lot longer than neuroscience and MRI scans, but it works on the same principles: that is why at the height of the experience you are asked to anchor that state with a small movement or gesture you can replicate with ease. You are building up good feelings.

The more good feelings you have about your capacity to do things well and get the outcomes you want, the more confident and capable you will feel about the next goals you undertake. And life tends to be a self-fulfilling prophecy – you get whatever you expect to get.

Try it now: Feel good now

Tell yourself: 'I want to feel good now, and this is how I am changing my thinking in order to do so.' Select the new beliefs to hold about your fabulous self and repeat them to yourself each day. For example:

✳ 'I feel happier because all tasks are easy and they don't take long to do now that I have developed easy strategies for doing them.'
✳ 'I trust my subconscious to be working for me.'
✳ 'I know that new work / clients / jobs are easy to come by.'

You will be amazed at how this simple exercise helps your confidence grow. Make up your mind to be happy now, see what you will see, hear what you will hear, luxuriate in the experience of feeling the feelings you will have when you have already achieved the outcomes you want. The more easily you can experience and visualize the things you want, the easier it is to attract these experiences into your life.

Focus points

In this chapter you will have learned:

* ❉ How values drive us and provide meaning in our lives
* ❉ How to align your goals and values
* ❉ To use values to increase your motivation and peak performance
* ❉ To anchor a 'feel good' state which you can use as a confidence builder.

Next step

Values are what drive you, give you passion, and provide your motivation in life. To know what is important to you, check your values. Match your motivation to your work and relationships. Align your values to the work you do. In the next chapter I will show you how to develop an understanding of what it means to have a purpose and thereby create a compelling future.

5

Find your purpose

In this chapter you will:

- ▶ *Understand the importance of discovering your own purpose*
- ▶ *Check how others align their goals with their purpose*
- ▶ *Gather your resources for being more aligned and purposeful*
- ▶ *Reflect on how your purposeful actions might benefit others.*

Whose purpose?

A solicitor had worked his way up the ladder to become a senior partner in his firm, yet he didn't feel either happy or successful. He had a wonderful home and family whom he adored and a good lifestyle – yet on most days he said he felt his achievements were empty and that he wanted to do something else. He, like many people, had worked really hard towards a purpose that was not his own but one his parents had chosen for him.

To 'be on your own purpose', your mind and body must know what *you* want, so that you can develop new types of behaviours that support your goals.

Try it now: Whose purpose?

Ask yourself the following questions and answer as honestly as you can:
* Is it time to change what you are doing?
* Did you choose the life you are living now? Or did someone else choose it for you?
* Or, did you fail to make a choice and just happened to end up where you are now by default?

Case study: Diana Gibbs, writer

'I turned down a chance to write a book because of family illness, lack of time, and the day job. However, the calling to write grew stronger in me and the sense of frustration I felt at not having submitted my outline when the series editor's offer was made would not go away.

'I felt so wretched I decided that if another offer came I would grab the chance and worry about how I would do the writing afterwards. I honed my writing skills so that I was ready for the call. The call came months later when I was approached at a conference by a publisher who was seeking authors to launch a new range of books – this time I jumped at the chance. Since then I have written books regularly, 15 of them, in spare time that I never believed I had. The real difference came when I realized one day that I had made the change – I was a writer. It was ingrained in me as part of my identity. And what writers do is write.'

'Tragedy in life doesn't lie in not reaching your goal – the tragedy lies in having no goal to reach.'

Benjamin Mays American minister and educator

Being 'on purpose'

Why is it that some people who possess what seem to be only average abilities achieve outstanding successes in life, while others with amazing talents achieve little? The answer is that being 'on purpose' is what counts – if you have a belief in a long-term purpose that you really care about and burn to make it happen, then all your thoughts, actions, achievements and goals will flow together towards realizing your dreams.

Remember this

People who have good self-esteem usually have a sense of purpose. Their sense of purpose connects with who they think they are and what is important to them. They link their beliefs and behaviours to their identity and then take the actions that propel them towards their desires.

Your key to success is to build a strong purpose that you care about, along with a passion strong enough to take you through the difficult times. The joys of being 'on purpose' are immeasurable. When you are purposeful and constantly motivated towards your target your senses are heightened and you feel truly alive. Purposeful people feed off the energy surges from remembered past successes to create bigger, bolder and more inspiring challenges to master. Confident they will succeed, they radiate an energy that is charismatic for others, who are drawn to their cocktail of vibrancy and action like moths towards a flame.

Passion is an indicator of what you value; it is what draws you, holds your attention and keeps you thinking late at night. It is the one thing you would do if you had all the money and resources that you needed. What work would *you* do for nothing?

Try it now: What do you feel passionate about?

Before deciding to make meaningful changes in your life you first have to identify what is important to you and whether it aligns with your values. Ask yourself:

✻ What makes me feel passionate?
✻ What makes me feel really good about the work I do?
✻ What is really important to me in my relationships?

Then ask yourself: 'Where can I start to make changes?'

The key to being 'on purpose'

Some people may say that their purpose in life is to make huge amounts of money, but money is only an exchange mechanism, a lifeless pile of paper to be exchanged for the feelings associated with having the things you desire. When you dig deep you find that a lot of what people want from wealth is changes in the way that they 'feel'.

Aristotle Onassis, the Greek shipping billionaire, when asked why he still worked so hard when he was fabulously rich, said: 'Because I never want to experience poverty again.' He was rich beyond most people's wildest dreams and yet it was a *feeling* that spurred him on to greater effort. He did not want to feel the fear he felt at the thought of losing all his wealth and being poor again. Onassis ran a very successful, 'away from pain' strategy.

This, I believe, is not a good model for a purposeful, and therefore happy, life. The key to being on purpose is in finding what you want to do.

Purpose brings energy, purpose brings focus, purpose brings new ways of thinking and feeling, and looking for ways to achieve your aims in life. Purpose comes from self-knowledge. So, here are some idea-sparking questions for you to answer. Write your answers down and think about what your answers reveal about your personal aptitudes and passions.

Try it now: Finding your purpose

Try to answer the following questions as fully as possible – perhaps as much as half a page per question. Allow yourself reflection time, so that you can probe quite deeply, rather than giving superficial answers off the top of your head.

❋ What are the activities that you were drawn to in childhood?
❋ What are the things that others say you are naturally good at?
❋ What are the things that you perform with ease?

Were you the child that liked listening, or the one that wanted to be watched? Are you a good communicator, a natural athlete? Do people say that you're a clown, or can you pick up on a situation quickly and effortlessly? Are you intuitive, or a born organizer, good in a crisis, sympathetic, or a persuasive speaker? The abilities and talents at which you excel are often indicators of where your life purpose lies – especially if you *enjoy* doing those things.

Have you achieved any successes in relation to the areas associated with your talents?

Case study: Pete Cohen

Anyone who's met Pete Cohen is immediately struck by his sense of purpose. Over the past 15 years this bestselling author and *GMTV* and *This Morning* resident life coach has helped thousands of people to lose weight, get fit and feel great about themselves.

Watching Pete perform, you might think that life has always been easy for him – but you'd be wrong. He was marked out from an early age as a low achiever. His teachers said he would never amount to anything and he left school at 16 with no qualifications. Later in life he was diagnosed as being severely dyslexic.

Pete achieved his aims by turning his teachers' negative predictions about him into a motivational tool that spurred him towards his dreams. He worked hard and now has an impressive list of qualifications in almost every aspect of sports and fitness training as well as coaching and remedial work.

His second motivation was self-belief. He says: 'I knew what I wanted so I spent plenty of time visualizing my success. I always knew exactly what it would look like and feel like. I knew that, however long it took, I would eventually succeed if I kept myself focused on the outcome I wanted. If you lose sight of your goal, it's easy to lose heart when times are tough.'

Try it now: What feeling do *you* want to have?

Imagine a future when you have already achieved your purpose. What feelings do you want to experience? Do you want a feeling of 'freedom', 'being loved', 'recognition', 'security' or some other kind of feeling? Do your feelings come mostly from having accumulated vast sums of money or are they tied in more closely to your personal achievements?

Purpose and values

Being on purpose is often closely allied to values (see Chapter 4). Having a purpose is not necessarily only self-serving (being famous, making money, even finding self-fulfilment); it can be about activating and building on those values you feel passionate about.

Case study: Leo Angart

Leo Angart's purpose is to let the world know that poor eyesight and wearing glasses is not an inevitable result of the ageing process. He corrected his own eyesight using energy exercises that he came across in a book and later he discovered the eye exercises pioneered by William Bates. By bringing in his own expertise in the field of hypnosis and healing, he has come up with a recipe for improving eyesight the natural way. He claims to have 20/20 vision and not to have worn glasses for six years.

He believes that children are often prescribed glasses wrongly and, once labelled as having poor eyesight, those children end up wearing spectacles for life. Leo says: 'Children's eyesight is constantly changing according to the tasks they are performing and their levels of health, nutrition and tiredness. Myopia is not a natural state. People from cultures with no written tradition don't suffer from short-sightedness. Yet when their children attend Western-style schools they stare at books and blackboards and develop myopia. Putting them in glasses is like putting a broken arm in plaster and then expecting that arm to get stronger – it doesn't; it gets weaker.'

Leo devised his vision workshops and now teaches children in Hong Kong how to relax and exercise their eyes. His Magic Eyes workshops are doing well in Mexico, Austria and Manila and his teaching methods are expanding into Moscow, Dubai and Brazil. He is shooting a video in the US which will be released in different languages, and there are even plans to introduce this type of training into the US Army.

Leo is only one of many motivated people who wake up knowing what they have to do each day and the steps they need to take towards achieving their goals in life. They know that the magic formula for personal success is to find a need that they care deeply about, and then to devise ways to satisfy it.

How does your purpose benefit others?

Try it now: How does your purpose benefit others?

✳ Is there a cause that you feel passionate about?
✳ Is there something that holds your attention because you care deeply about it?
✳ Could your life purpose be based around it?
✳ Write your answers down – because, like mining for diamonds, somewhere in there is the key to finding your purposeful direction in life.

By focusing on their vision, motivated people create a model in their minds of what success looks like, then their imagination kicks into action to create compelling ideas that propel them towards their goals. This doesn't mean that they won't fail at times, but their happiness does not depend on external circumstances – their purpose is strong enough to carry them through the difficult times.

Modelling strategies

All human behaviour, including yours, is based on strategies, which are reproducible. By understanding how your own and other people's strategies work, you can learn to reproduce the ones you want at will. If you want to excel at something, you can model someone else's behaviour in order to enhance the skills you need to achieve your goals.

Below is an example of how a teacher has modelled a spelling strategy used by people who spell excellently, and then taught the strategy to adults and children who can't spell.

Case study: Cricket Kemp

Cricket Kemp's purpose is to help people spell. She runs 'magical spelling days' for children, teachers and adult non-spellers. In one of her sessions she teaches a spelling strategy used by excellent spellers. Cricket's passion is to make a difference to the lives of children and adults by teaching them a spelling strategy that works for them.

Cricket says, 'I started to experiment to discover how you could teach the spelling strategy to people who didn't naturally hold it, or who had difficulty learning to spell, by getting them to use a visual process.

'This has resulted in an elaboration of a Robert Dilts strategy which he pioneered in Californian schools, and in many new strategies for teaching spelling. Most children who learn the strategy increase their reading age by an average of 13 months within three months – a result which is off the scale for reading improvement schemes.' She goes on to say: 'When you notice people's patterns for doing something well the pattern can be evaluated, tested, taught and learned. This is really useful because it allows us to accumulate information and pass it on.'

By observing what good spellers do when they are spelling and what people who can't spell are doing when they attempt to spell, Cricket noticed that good spellers almost always use a visual spelling strategy; to learn new words, they imagine seeing the word in their mind's eye. Typically, people who couldn't spell or who were poor spellers attempted to learn to spell using auditory methods – saying the word out loud and then repeating it in their heads.

In Cricket's case success and purpose do not necessarily translate into making money: 'It is also about what brings meaning into people's lives.'

Align your actions with your beliefs, purpose, values and goals

Purpose comes from knowing that the things you do align with your beliefs and values.

Values are things which are important to you. You may value good manners, good service, punctuality or people telling you the truth. And, mostly, you can see whether these values are being upheld.

Beliefs are different from values. You can believe things that are not actually true. You can believe that your house is safe, until it's flooded or the ceiling falls in. You can believe that you have a happy relationship until your partner tells you he or she is leaving you. At this point you start to re-examine your beliefs about how safe your house is or how good your relationship was.

Whole groups of people or nations can share the same beliefs. The American nation believed it was invincible until terrorists flew two planes into the World Trade Center. At times like this, when a disaster happens, people have the painful task of re-examining what they had believed to be true – in order to know what they now believe.

Key idea

Beliefs, values and purpose are our drivers. These are the things that motivate us and make us who we are. If you don't know what drives you, you cannot motivate yourself or press your own 'hot' buttons so that you can be more effective at getting the results you want from life.

Remember this

When you know your values, then live by them.

Try it now: Build a dream future based on your values

List your six uppermost values from the group you collected in Chapter 4 and spend some time reflecting on how you can build a dream that reflects your most important values.

The formula for finding out what you really want to do is:

✸ Identify what is important to you
✸ Clarify what you want
✸ Decide which changes to make.

All of this means nothing unless you take follow-up actions. Plant these seeds in your mind:

- ▶ 'What steps can I take today to lead me nearer to my goal?'

- ▶ 'What are the actions I can take that will give me leverage?'

- ▶ 'What is the next action I can take today to make the future I want a reality?' It may be small but whatever it is – do it.

Your purpose, beliefs, values and destiny are all intertwined. As your thoughts and actions flow together and your energy for your purpose builds, you will find that opportunities open up for you in often unexpected ways. It may be a chance meeting, a proposal, a snatch of someone's conversation that alerts your senses and calls you to take actions that propel you towards your goals.

Focus points:

By the end of this chapter you will have:

 ✳ Learned whose purpose you are presently on, your own or someone else's
 ✳ Recognized that passion is an indicator of what is important to you
 ✳ Explored the key to being on purpose
 ✳ Reflected on how your purposeful actions might benefit others.

Next step

Don't think too much about how fortunate you were to be in the right place at the right time. Just remember you have served your apprenticeship and it was meant to happen. You don't have time to labour over how you got your break. Just be joyous that you knew your purpose, and trust that this is another link towards your ultimate destination. You paid for your ticket with all the effort and purpose that has brought you to this point. In the next chapter you will gather thinking tools to help you generate even better solutions. Be joyful!

6

Sharpen your thinking – generate better solutions

In this chapter you will:

▶ *Gather thinking tools that help you generate better solutions*

▶ *Use Walt Disney's creativity strategy*

▶ *Look for people who already have the strategies you want to possess*

▶ *Explore success strategies that give greater leverage towards reaching goals*

▶ *Discover flexible thinking that lets you view situations from different angles.*

'When I was working on the Theory of Relativity, I was no Einstein.'

Albert Einstein

I watched a TV programme called *Superhumans* where finalists were challenged to demonstrate their most fantastic capabilities. One finalist could say which day of the week any date given to him fell on, in any period over the last 500 years. He was able to give the correct answers to 100 random dates in under two minutes. The eventual winner of *Superhumans* was able to solve ten Rubik's Cube puzzles in two minutes. These were truly superhuman feats. It was calculated that only one in 7 billion people was ever likely to have these capabilities.

Both 'superhumans' were running internal sequencing strategies, which neuroscientists were able to unravel by using MRI scans while watching which part of their brains lit up as they thought through their tasks. The runner-up who was able to name the day of the week a date fell on was running an algorithm. The winner who solved the Rubik's Cubes did so by colour pattern recognition, and converting the colours into letters, then stringing letters together to make word combinations he memorized. These people really were 'superhuman'!

Many of the people we hail as geniuses are simply clever people who have developed strategies for doing things incredibly well. Human beings have limited brainpower; there is only so much we can remember and learn. However, we have abilities for pattern recognition and for inventing tools, devices and strategies that expand our capabilities.

Edward de Bono's 'Thinking Course' in the 1980s taught thinking as a skill, using simple but powerful strategies and questions as tools to optimize thinking. Many countries' school curriculums adopted his courses, and taught their people how to think by giving children thinking and problem-solving strategies.

Key idea

If you live in a country where schools do not teach thinking strategies, here is a question to ask yourself: 'Who taught me how to think?' If you taught yourself, or you copied your parents or peers, then ask yourself: 'Do I have the best thinking tools I could possess?' and 'Are there bits of the learning processes that might have been left out?'

In this chapter we will, like De Bono, explore a range of thinking questions and strategies for achieving the outcomes we want.

Gathering other people's strategies

Let's start by looking at three strategies for refining your thinking skills, all pioneered by well-known and successful personalities.

Try it now: Collect – and then assess – other people's strategies

Collect strategies from the people around you who already have the skills you want to acquire. This is an immensely useful tool because, if you can spot someone who already has the strategy you want, you are two-thirds of the way towards having it yourself. It does not have to be your work colleagues – it can be people you hear in radio or TV interviews or famous people in the news as well. Sources of new thinking strategies are all around you – so open your eyes and ears! Read through the rest of this chapter first, then list some strategies that would be useful for you to acquire. As you do this, think about the following:

❋ What would each of these strategies let you do that you cannot do now?
❋ What might having these new techniques give you leverage towards achieving?

TONY BUZAN'S MIND MAPS

Tony Buzan devised the idea of mind maps, a colourful visual form of note-taking that lets people capture and explore aspects of their thinking that might otherwise escape them were they to use conventional, linear note-taking. The maps contain a central idea or image, and themes are explored by following branches that radiate from it.

The technique is a cleverly simple tool that expands the range of things that people can do. Mapping is useful for brainstorming new ideas, which can then be explored by following the branches that connect to the central theme.

WALT DISNEY'S DREAMER/REALIST/CRITIC STRATEGY

Another technique was developed by Walt Disney, hailed as a genius for his breath-taking cartoon films such as *Fantasia*, *Bambi* and Sleeping *Beauty*. Disney used the following strategy to take his teams through creative processes, such as developing storylines, to ensure that dialogue and animation fitted perfectly:

1 **The Dreamer stage** When you are brainstorming for new ideas, act as if you are the most knowledgeable person in the world. Disney had different rooms for different types of thinking, and during the Dreamer stage – designed to convey a starburst of ideas – no one was allowed to criticize anyone's input.

2 **The Realist stage** At this stage people work out what is possible – in terms of theme, form and structure – and flesh out the outline. This is the practical stage from which the first draft emerges.

3 **The Critic stage** When the realist stage is finished the inner critic steps in. At this point you become the most critical person in the world and look to find the flaws in your creation.

Disney's tripartite strategy can be used by anyone to improve the quality of ideas they generate, articles they write, books they structure, and concepts or products they are planning to launch.

Next time you are planning something important, try it and see whether this strategy improves your outcome.

I use Disney's technique for feature writing when brainstorming for ideas at the kitchen table. During the Dreamer phase, there is a whiteboard on the wall so I can capture good ideas. For the Realist stage I move on to the computer and input structure and comb through my work to get it into shape. At the final Critic stage I stand at the polished kitchen worktop and read my copy aloud as if I am another, more critical person. At this stage, I can hear my 'inner' editor commenting and telling me what changes to make. Then it's back to the computer to hone the feature and send it off.

Using the Disney strategy gives you a means to improve the quality of everything you do before submitting your project to other people for more critical inspection.

Remember this

If someone else can do something, all they have is a better strategy than the one you are currently using. Use their technique and develop the skill.

GERALD FORD'S 'KILLER QUESTION'

This strategy is especially useful when making decisions under pressure.

In 1976 Gerald Ford was President of the US and he was faced with a massive decision – whether or not to inoculate the population of America against swine flu. There was evidence for a predicted major flu epidemic as virulent as the 1918 flu strain that killed half a million Americans. Scientists predicted that this virus would kill 1 million people.

Ford was faced with a landscape of puzzling and changing information. He had bits of the jigsaw, but not all of the pieces, and incoming information arrived each day that altered the scenario.

The President could not wait for an epidemic to happen, or have the luxury of making decisions with hindsight. He had to decide whether to inoculate the population of America or not based on the information that was at hand. If he inoculated the population and nothing happened, then his efforts would be seen as a huge, wasteful and costly exercise. If he did nothing and many people contracted the illness and died, he would be accused of not doing enough to protect the US population.

Ford designed a killer question, the answer to which would give him as near a recipe for certainty as anyone can get in uncertain situations.

The final question Ford worked with was:

> *'Is there any fresh information from any source that would cause me to rethink my decision? And does such evidence exist?'*

The question is useful if you are under pressure to make decisions when the information you have is incomplete and the outcome uncertain. It is useful for deciding if it is time to quit your job, ideal if attending meetings run by strong individuals who may have their own agenda, or in companies where 'group think' rules. It is best used before a final decision is taken and can be applied to any topic big or small as it brings a new way of thinking to an established frame.

Gerald Ford's question is a fantastic tool because it cuts through people's fixed agendas or narrow focused thinking and causes them to reflect again. Simply uttering the words can spark new thinking at a point when all likely alternatives seem exhausted. It works equally well on small decision-making tasks and larger-scale decisions such as whether to invade another country, where the consequences of getting things wrong can be devastating.

Try it now: Ask the killer question

1 Think of a personal situation that you would benefit from having more insight into. It might be 'How do I change my situation to something better?' 'Will I / won't I take this risk?' 'Where can I find the resources to help me start my project?'
2 Then ask: 'Is there any fresh information from any source that would cause me to rethink my decision? And does such evidence exist?'
3 What have you learned that you did not know before?

Gerald Ford's thinking frame gives you an overview on a situation. It is a high-level questioning of your actions that adds objectivity to your thinking and can be asked at the end of any thinking-through process. Asking the question will generate more options on the likely implications of the action you are about to take.

Key idea: We never fully develop all our talents

No matter what age we are, we all have talents that are not fully developed. Successful people realize that they are the only people who can improve their results, so they plan ahead. They start with a goal in the future to aim for and then devise a plan of action by systematically thinking backwards to the present time and working out what resources, skills, abilities, tools and techniques they will require to achieve their aim.

Chunking

In this second part of the chapter I want to look at a really useful NLP thinking strategy – chunking. Think of this as a handy piece of software, ready to install in your brain.

Key idea: Seven, plus or minus two

In 1956 the cognitive psychologist George Miller discovered that the average number of objects, or pieces of information, the average human being could hold in their working memory is seven, plus or minus two.

Giving people tasks with more than this amount of information causes memory overload and reduces their capacity to concentrate, manipulate and deal with information. That is why, when things get difficult and you can't see the whole structure of a plan, it is most helpful to chunk the information down. Then concentrate on one small section at a time.

'Chunking' is a process of grouping information into large or small amounts – 'chunks' – depending on the type of information we want to obtain.

▶ **To chunk up** when thinking means to go from small detail-specific questions such as 'How specifically will I...?' to big-picture thinking that involves how the whole process or project works.

▶ **To chunk down** is to go from seeing the finished project, the big picture, to homing in on individual aspects, small component parts that form part of the whole. Chunking down large objectives into smaller goals makes them easier to deal with.

Having the flexibility to chunk your thinking or questions up or down in any situation is one of the most valuable skills you can acquire. Chunking helps you organize your thinking so you can handle more information in different ways.

Situations where having the flexibility to chunk your thinking up and down at will is useful include:

▶ goal setting

▶ negotiating

▶ team building

▶ motivating people

▶ resolving conflict

▶ intervening in situations, to find out at what level to intervene

▶ focusing on one aspect of a situation

▶ problem solving.

The most able thinkers are skilled in changing their thinking patterns at will in order to ask questions that shed light on a task, situation, event, project or outcome in lots of different ways. This type of thinking lets you gain more insight into situations from seeing a subject from lots of different points of view.

Case study: Thelma

How do you know it is time to chunk down? Often it is a feeling that tells you it is time to chunk your thinking up or down. Thelma got a 'feeling' like a dark heavy cloud over the back part of the left side of her brain each time she felt stressed and had to complete tasks to deadline. First came the feeling, then she saw pictures of lots of pages of paper in front of her face so that they obscured her view. Each paper represented a different project, and it made her feel as if the work was never-ending, and that she could never focus entirely on just one piece of work.

I asked Thelma to imagine that each project was a sheet of paper laid out in a neat row from left to right on the floor and then asked how she could use this image to help her feel less stressed. Thelma said that what would motivate her was if she could choose just one sheet of paper labelled with the 'project name' at a time, and bring the image close enough to be within her vision, but not enough to block her view. She would focus on only one task at a time, make sure she knew the procedure for doing the task before starting, and give herself a reward for completing it on time.

Thelma was chunking her thinking and tasks down.

Remember this: Chunk your images when you need motivation

If you cannot get around to doing a task you really know you should, ask yourself:

▶ 'What are the "pictures" and "feelings" I associate around doing this task?'

▶ 'How can I change them and make them more motivating for me?'

▶ What size chunks do I want my information served in, so they are the right-sized bites for me?'

DEVELOPING FLEXIBLE THINKING SKILLS

You do not need to reinvent the wheel and devise your own tools – simply find out who can do it and then learn their strategies. To become a flexible thinker capable of focusing on the 'big picture' or whole plan in one instant and 'small detail-specific' information in another, it is important that we can 'chunk' our thinking up and down at will. 'Big picture' thinking will let us see what the whole project will look like when it is finished. Setting your objectives requires that you change your thinking and begin to think in detail about how each of your objectives will be met.

Remember this

You already know how to chunk information – you do it when you remember phone numbers. You group the regional part of the number together and then split the rest of the numbers into chunks to make them more memorable.

▶ How to chunk up your thinking

To chunk up for solutions to 'big picture' outcomes, ask questions that require people to examine their beliefs, values and what is important to them.

Think about a situation you would like to change, move on from, or resolve. Ask yourself:

▶ 'What is important to me about...?'

▶ 'What would motivate me to ...?'

▶ 'What does having this outcome achieve for me?'

▶ 'And for what purpose?'

Chunking up skills are vital for analysing problems and finding out the 'why' of what is important. Chunking up helps you find the best approach to new situations and for setting new and more challenging goals.

▶ How to chunk down your thinking

To chunk down so that you can find out about specific outcomes, ask questions that elicit small detail explanations.

Think about a situation that you might be avoiding that is stopping you taking action and moving ahead. Ask yourself:

▶ 'What stops me...?'

▶ 'What is an example of this?'

▶ 'Who/what/when/where/how ... specifically?'

To recap:

▶ When you have a problem that seems daunting, think of chunking it down into smaller, more manageable sections. This enables you to focus on one specific area at a time and find solutions, before moving on to the next task.

▶ If you are feeling overwhelmed by too much detail, then chunk up to find the purpose or meaning for what you are doing. Getting the big picture will give you an overview so you can define your purpose, what you are doing and why you need to do it.

► Chunking enables you to view situations from different angles.

► Chunking skills build flexible thinking, which is vital for analysing problems, finding the best approach to new situations and setting new and more challenging goals. You can also use your chunking skills to help people consider which chunk sizes are best suited for the tasks they want to achieve.

Remember this:

'The law of requisite variety' states that in any given interaction, the system (or person) with the widest range of (thinking and doing) options will be the one that wins the day.

Focus points

By the end of this chapter you will have:

* Gathered thinking tools to help you generate better solutions
* Understood Walt Disney's creativity strategy
* Tried out Gerald Ford's 'killer question' on your own situation
* Know how to chunk your thinking up and down at will.

Next step

Questions to ask to move a person from the small detail to the 'big picture' outcomes are ones that require people to examine their beliefs, values and what is important to them. Once you know your purpose, you can build your motivation; once you have a store of strategies, you can use them to perfect your techniques in whatever you want to do, and you can move further forward faster. In the next chapter we will discover whether there are any blocks that might impede your success, and learn whether your 'inner team members' are all routing for you.

7

Motivating your inner team

In this chapter you will:

▶ *Learn whether your inner team members are all routing for you*

▶ *Identify specific inner gremlins and their assigned tasks*

▶ *Select your inner team cheerleaders – those with beliefs who support you*

▶ *'Send off' unhelpful members to reduce the power of inner criticism*

▶ *Add some structure to your thinking using the NLP logical levels of thinking.*

Are your inner team members really working for you?

Inside us we have lots of different components that make up our inner team and contribute to the way we think. We might have a team member who says: 'I wake up each day and I feel good, and I expect good things to happen.' We may have another part of us who alerts us to things that are coming up in the future who says: 'We must be prepared in case something unexpected happens.' We may have another team member who takes care of our welfare and says: 'It's time we took a holiday.'

There may be other team members who, although trying to help us, actually undermine us. We may have parts of us that say: 'I can't do this – I will never get it right' or 'It's time for me to panic.' Their purpose is to help us and keep us safe and away from imminent failure, but the other function they unintentionally perform is to stop us reaching our full potential and being successful.

Try it now: Does your inner team work for or against you?

Do you have an inner critic who tells you that you cannot do things? Is there an inner voice that says one of the following?

* 'I must please other people.'
* 'I must hurry up.'
* 'I must be perfect.'
* 'I am not good enough.'
* 'I could never do that.'

Circle any of the inner critic team members that apply to you and write down how each affects you, for good as well as for bad. For example: 'I must be perfect. That is why I procrastinate and finish things late – the good thing is that when I do finish the job is done just right!'

A team member can be helpful as well as unhelpful. A part of you that says 'I must be perfect in everything I do' can, on a good level, help you to achieve many of the things you strive for. They may be valuable to you and worth 9 out of 10. The same team member who strives too hard for perfection and sees nothing you do as good enough can also instil a sort of paralysis in you. This may result in your thinking a lot, but not actually doing anything in case you get it wrong. This team member, although they want your best behaviour, is actually undermining your outcomes. They might score a 0 out of 10 and be worth relegating in favour of another player.

Try it now: Rank your team members

Rank your team member(s) as to how helpful they are to you on a continuum line of 0 to 10, where 1 is an ineffective result and 10 is a good result.

Your self-confidence and the gremlins that undermine it

Self-confidence relates to actions and how we view ourselves when we perform those actions. If we feel confident when facing an unfamiliar or difficult task, we will expect to perform well. We review our memories of how we tackled new challenges in the past, and if we feel that we performed them well then we carry those confident feelings with us and expect that our success patterns will repeat themselves.

Try it now: Identify your gremlins

1 Think back to the last two events where you attempted to achieve something – for example you had a difficult conversation with someone, took a test, did some public speaking. Choose things that were significant for you and where the event did not go well. Revisit the experiences afresh so that you can gain some new insight into the experience.
2 Quickly play each event again, leaving out the content, and just listening to your own inner comments about what was happening.
3 Identify if you were running any of your inner critical voices.
4 Play the second negative experience, so that you can identify your thinking behaviour patterns, and they things you say to yourself when things are not going well.

What have you learned about how your inner gremlins support or undermine you at critical times because of what they say about your abilities to achieve your aims?

To feel supremely confident, we need to hold a store of strong mental images of seeing ourselves doing phenomenally well at the tasks we undertake. If we do not hold strong images of our successful outcomes, then we may be more prone to fail, even though there may be evidence to suggest that we have the same skills and experience as people around us who expect to do well.

Remember this

We undermine our ability to perform tasks well when we have low self-confidence.

Self-assessment: How confident are you?

Answer the following questions as honestly as you can:

1 Can you accept a compliment gracefully, without saying 'it was nothing' or something else that will lessen the impact?

2 Are you afraid that a success was a one-off and that somebody might find you out as not being as good as they think?

3 Can you list six qualities you like about yourself without hesitating?

4 How well do you react when asked to try something you have not done before?

5 What do you say to yourself when you are about to do something difficult or challenging?

Do your answers suggest your inner team members are all supporting you?

SIGNS OF LOW SELF-CONFIDENCE

Think about the things you constantly say to yourself about new situations or tasks you consider strange or difficult. Do any of the following common undermining beliefs keep coming up?

Thinking

► 'I can't do it – I wouldn't know where to start.'

► 'It is too difficult for me.'

- ► 'I don't think I can handle this.'
- ► 'What I do won't be good enough – other people can do things better.'

Feeling

- ► Worried or anxious and not knowing why
- ► Apprehension about future difficulties
- ► Being frustrated and angry with yourself
- ► Fear of the unknown or of new situations
- ► Anger because other people seem to find things so easy to do
- ► Discouraged and demoralized

Behaviour

- ► Seeking reassurance
- ► Not participating, but staying in the background
- ► Hesitation and repeatedly needing others to say you are doing all right
- ► Avoiding taking on new situations, or making changes in your life
- ► Procrastinating, or being a slow starter
- ► Passive, waiting to be told what to do, not a self-starter

Try it now: Decide which team members can stay and which need to be replaced

1 Think back to the last couple of situations when you did not do well. Write down the things you were saying to yourself about what was going on in your mind. List the things you said to yourself that supported you. List the things you said to yourself that undermined your confidence.

2 On a piece of paper, draw a line down the centre. Reflect on the thoughts and the things you most constantly say to yourself while you work, during testing experiences or in difficult social/relationship situations. Decide which team member is advising you or telling you what to do and give them a name that describes their job role – for example 'team organizer' or 'pessimist'. Use the following list to help you:

Thought	Role
'I will do it!'	Inner cheerleader
'I am a good team member.'	Inner cheerleader
'I must hurry up!'	Team organizer
'Here's how I will do it differently next time.'	Inner strategist
'I will never do it!'	Inner critic
'I can't get it right!'	Underminer
'It is all my fault (or someone else's fault).'	Blamer
'I will never get the chance.'	Pessimist

3 Now look at your team and decide which members you want to keep, which members you want to replace, and which new members you want to bring on to your team. Write a list of the qualities of each:

   ▷ 'Team members I will keep are my...'
   ▷ 'List of qualities each member brings that support me...'
   ▷ 'Team members I want to replace are my...'
   ▷ 'List of qualities each member brings that do not support me...'
   ▷ 'New team members I will add are...'
   ▷ 'List of qualities each new member brings that support me...'

Remember that *all* of your inner team members do the best they can for you, regardless of how helpful or unhelpful their words. For example: 'Procrastinator' may have saved you from failing at anything because you never completed anything in time, so nobody judged you as having failed. When replacing such team members, try to come up with the type of thinking that would support you and be more helpful to you. You might replace, for instance, Procrastinator with a team member who says 'The task does not have to be perfect – I just need to get the job done!'

Actively work to replace each unhelpful team member with another member with the type of thinking that would help you crack on and bring about a positive change for you.

4 Finally, select a cheerleader – someone in your corner cheering you on. Whom do you know who has these qualities? It might be a television coach or personality, or a person whom you have seen enable others around you. Select that person as your inner cheerleader and remember what they say to their charges that supports them when they get things wrong.

Case study: Howard

Howard was a project manager for a large telecommunications firm. He knew he was good at coming up with ideas that worked and implementing them. Yet when he presented his ideas, they were often dismissed in what seemed to him a perfunctory manner.

Howard's self-confidence was shaken: 'I can feel myself "shrink" as I get nearer to head office and feel "diminished" as I open the meeting-room door.' He noticed that other people who were more enthusiastic about their ideas seemed to get them accepted, and realized that, while his ideas were 'strong' enough, they simply needed to be presented with confidence and a bit of razzmatazz.

How we see and feel about ourselves affects our self-confidence in any situation from boardroom to bedroom. For Howard, what he enjoyed most and made him feel most powerful was being on his own driving in his car, when he played loud, rousing classical music that engaged his emotions. This made him feel powerful: 'When I get out of the car after a burst of music I feel strong and able to deal with anything.'

Because music engaged his strongest emotions and made him feel in control, he decided to use it as a way of managing his state when he entered the meeting. As he drove to his firm's head office, he would listen to the music and imagine himself conducting an orchestra. As he did so, he would visualize running through his presentation to the board a couple of times while his appreciative audience nodded their heads enthusiastically and applauded.

Howard decided that his inner team members would comprise his orchestra and he would be the 'conductor'. When he waved his baton his team members would work in harmony towards his goals. He dropped some members of his orchestra – his inner critic, for example – and replaced them with better players!

Within two presentations Howard could see that his ideas were now being discussed and adopted with enthusiasm. There was also a change in the way the board engaged with him; there was now more banter and goodwill. Howard reflects: 'On a logical level, I already knew my ideas were good but the change in the board's acceptance of them only came after I dropped my inner critic so I could be excited without feeling inhibited.'

We can strengthen our sense of self-confidence by choosing new strategies for doing things we particularly want to achieve, and holding strong images of ourselves performing tasks particularly well. If we do this often enough, we will automatically begin to see ourselves as natural born winners at everything we do.

Try it now: Get yourself a cheerleader

If you hold any of the limiting beliefs in the left-hand column below, think about how you might bombard you inner team member who holds that belief with so much evidence to the contrary that they give up in favour of an alternative, more positive belief. Get yourself a cheerleader from the positive right-hand column to take their place.

Negative team's belief	Positive team's belief
Failing at anything is painful	'I can do that! It doesn't have to be perfect – just get it done!'
'I can't do this.'	'I am good at this; I just don't know it yet.'
'I am no good at this.'	'I achieve what I set out to do! Can I apply a strategy that will make me even better?'
'I always get things wrong.'	'I allow time to do things, and list my resources so I can see them at a glance.'
'I am too fat/thin/short/tall/unhealthy.'	'I like being me.'
'I must do it all myself.'	'I ask for help and many people are prepared to help me.'
'I am afraid of meeting new people – they may not like me.'	'Strangers are just friends I have not been introduced to yet.'

ANCHOR A GOOD FEELING

Howard used the powerful technique of anchoring all the positive beliefs he had in order to anchor a good feeling to what would normally be a stressful situation. By taking all the images, sounds and feelings of joy and heightened awareness that he recalled vividly and attaching those feelings to a situation about which he felt apprehensive and did not enjoy, he changed his frame of thinking to one where he was confident and upbeat and expected to have his ideas accepted.

The words Howard used indicated not just how he felt about the situation but also how he held a picture of the problem in his mental landscape. People unconsciously describe the colour, clarity, size, shape or density of the picture they see in their mind's eye. They may talk of 'having a bright future', 'a dark cloud hanging over them', feeling as if they were 'wading through treacle' or 'walking on air'. These patterns of description for the most part go unnoticed, yet they are familiar enough to us that we recognize when they are out of place. You don't, for instance, hear people saying they are looking forward to a 'dim and distant future'.

Key idea: Describe your world more colourfully

Each person is unique in the way they see the world, but a pattern we tend to follow is that we give clarity, colour and nearness to things to which we feel strong emotional attachment. Things that are less interesting we send to the dark, dim, distant and hazy pictures box. We describe people we like as 'colourful' and 'larger than life', and those in whom we feel less interested in as 'drab' or 'colourless', as 'a grey little man in a suit'.

Changing how you view yourself and making the event seem more colourful can enhance your performance and ability to achieve your aims.

To achieve peak performance in a situation that makes you nervous, anchor a good feeling. An anchor is any stimulus that changes your state. (Remember Pavlov and how his dogs salivated when they heard the bell?) Anchors are fired when we think of associations or past successes when doing things we enjoyed or did well, which made us feel good about ourselves. By remembering a time when we did something particularly well and felt good about our performance, we can harness that good feeling and carry it with us when we enter a more challenging situation.

Use anchors when:

▶ you are in a situation that puts you under pressure

▶ you want to feel confident and draw on your inner resources

▶ you find you are responding in a familiar way that did not achieve good results before, and you want to change the way you feel and respond

We gain confidence and our sense of self-esteem increases when we build up images of ourselves engaging in actions that may be challenging and excelling at what we do. The more good experiences you can anchor and use in potentially difficult situations to overcome them, the more powerful the anchor becomes and the more successful you feel.

Try it now: Thinking strategy

1 Think of yourself undertaking your next challenging task, but this time with some of your new positive-thinking inner team members working with you. Act as if you already have them embedded in your thinking and they are working towards your goals.

2 Notice what phrases of encouragement they are saying to you that induce you to perform at your best.

3 Then see yourself performing new tasks effortlessly and incredibly well.

What is different about the scenario now?

Add structure to your thinking using the NLP 'logical levels'

Would it help if you could acquire a systematic way of thinking and problem solving that helped you expand your habitual thinking patterns? The NLP 'logical levels of change' model is a good way to help you discover your own, and other people's, underlying thinking patterns in relation to any event or occurrence. By understanding from what logical level a person is talking to you from, you have the chance to build rapport and engage more deeply with them in conversation.

Being able to think flexibly and at lots of different levels on a subject provides us with a powerful framework for thinking through change. We can problem-solve, uncover hidden information and gather extra insights about a situation from several different viewpoints and build up a 'big picture' view of events. We can think situations through on a different level or category at a time, and capture additional insights that would otherwise have escaped us.

There are five main logical levels:

1	ENVIRONMENT	Where something happens; a place or a context in which a behaviour occurs or repeats itself.
2	BEHAVIOUR	What we or someone else did.
3	CAPABILITY	How we, or someone, did, or should do, something.
4	BELIEFS AND VALUES	Why we should do something, and what we believe is and is not possible for us.
5	IDENTITY	Who we think we are and how we fit into a bigger system. This can be spiritual and takes us into exploring our bigger purpose and mission in the world.

In Figure 7.1 you can see how the levels are connected with one another. A change in a belief made at one level will influence other areas of your thinking. The effect is like throwing a large stone into a pond and seeing the ripples spread out.

Logical levels can help us clarify the way we see a situation, and reveal what are the real blocks and issues behind a situation. The core questions to ask are 'Who?', 'What?' 'Where?', 'When?', 'Why?' and 'How?'.

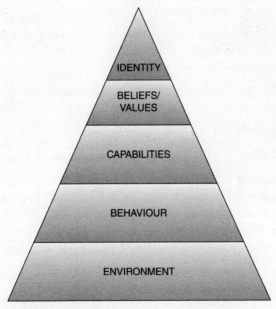

Figure 7.1 The five main logical levels

▶ **Environment: 'Where?' and 'When?'**

▷ Where and when does this situation occur? Is it a place, at work, at home, with colleagues?

▷ What is the setting and context within which the problem arises?

▶ **Behaviour: 'What is happening?'**

▷ What is being done, by whom, to whom?

▷ Equally, what is *not* being done? Is this about inactivity?

▶ **Capability: 'How is this being done?'**

▷ Capability is about how someone does something, or how confident they feel about doing it.

▷ Having capabilities is what makes people feel competent and in control of situations.

▷ If you feel you lack capabilities, you may find a task really difficult.

▶ **Beliefs and values: 'Why?'**

▷ Our beliefs and values are personal to us, and what we think shapes our understanding of what we believe is or is not possible for us.

▷ Beliefs and values provide us with a rationale and drive our actions.

▶ **Identity: 'Who?'**

▷ Who do you think you are? This is your identity.

▷ All your actions derive from your sense of who you are. You will hear people say, 'I am not the kind of person who does that...' or 'I am a good guy'. These people are telling you who they think they are.

Key idea: What do logical levels let us do

* Choosing to think a situation through on each of the logical levels helps us clarify our thinking about ourselves, our friends and colleagues, our workplace or any other entity with which we engage.
* The logical levels can let us work as a team to recognize on what level we need to concentrate in order to make breakthroughs.
* The logical levels build flexibility in our thinking by letting us explore a situation from each of the neurological levels. We learn things we might not otherwise have uncovered.

A simple example shows how useful it can be to clarify on what logical level someone is speaking from:

'I am a smoker.'	The person making this statement is telling you that smoking is part of their identity. It is who they are.	IDENTITY
'I smoke.'	The person making this statement is telling you what they do. They are describing a behaviour.	BEHAVIOUR

The distinction can be crucial. If you are a therapist charged with helping people to give up smoking, it will be much easier to help someone to give up what they see as an unwanted behaviour, which is on a lower logical level, than it will be to help someone who sees smoking as part of their identity, that is who they are.

Here's another example. You might hear someone say: 'On one level, not passing any exams was terrible; on another level I would never have built my own successful business if I could have got a paying job. It made me who I am.'

In one sentence, a person has discussed their thinking on different logical levels:

They did not pass their exams.	CAPABILITIES
They would never have built a successful business, if they could have got a paying job.	BELIEFS
They see themselves as a successful business owner. ('It made me who I am.')	IDENTITY

Key idea: Never be stuck for a fresh viewpoint again

Using logical levels means we do not need to be stuck or limited to our own regular way of thinking again. We can use the logical levels thinking frame to step outside our viewpoint and explore the situation with new eyes.

Try it now: Work through a problem using the logical levels

1. Think of a problem you would like to work through, or a situation concerning yourself or others in which you feel constrained and would like to clarify. Define the problem in one sentence, using this structure: *'I want to do…, but I can't because…'*

2. Take six pieces of paper and write the five logical levels on each one (Environment, Behaviour, etc.).

3. Space these pieces of paper on the floor and stand in front of each one in turn, starting with Environment.

4. For each heading ask the relevant questions from the list below. Ask the questions aloud and wait for the answers to come to you. Get used to having regular open dialogue with your inner self, and gaining information on every level on how you feel about situations.

Environment
▶ Where are you when you engage in this area of your life?
▶ What do you see and hear?

Behaviour
▶ What do you do (activities) when you engage in this area of your life?
▶ If someone was watching you, what would they see you do?
▶ What would they hear you say?

Capabilities
▶ What capabilities do you tap into in this area of your life?
▶ What skills do you put into becoming proactive?
▶ What areas of expertise do you draw on?

Beliefs and values

- What's important to you about doing/wanting/having this?
- Why does it matter?
- What's most important about it?

Identity

- Who are you in this area of your life?
- Who are you at your best in this area of your life?

5 Work your way through the logical levels of thinking up to Identity. Then go back and pause at each level, gathering up the new insights and information you collected at each stage and carrying it with you to the next.

6 By the end of the logical levels thinking process you will have insights into your situation that you did not have when you started.

Remember this: What logical levels thinking enables you to do

By questioning your thinking and beliefs about a topic, using one of the logical level questions (above) at a time, you can find out more about a situation and how someone thinks about it than you could otherwise have done. You can ascertain:

- what *sort of information* you are dealing with, whether it is about the person's environment, behaviour, capabilities, beliefs or identity
- from what level a person views a problem *originating*, whether it is about the environment, behaviour, capabilities, beliefs or identity
- on what level the problem is being *experienced*
- what the *real issue* is about.

Recognizing flashpoints

Sometimes when we have what seems to be a small disagreement with someone over something that seems trivial, it escalates into a major fallout. You may have watched the cartoon characters Homer and Marge Simpson as they argue with each other from different levels of thinking or points of view.

> Marge points out that Homer has left his socks on the bedroom floor:
>
> **Homer:** 'What's the matter with you? It is only a pair of socks.'
>
> (Homer sees situation as an *environmental* one about socks being in the wrong place.)
>
> **Marge:** 'No, you're always leaving your clothes on the floor for someone else to pick up. Who do you think you are?'
>
> (Marge is arguing on an *identity* level, and attaches his behaviour to the type of person she believes he is.)

People are often afraid to challenge another person's identity because it may end in conflict. We tend to start with something small, on an environment level, and if an argument ensues, proceed through the logical levels by taking the behaviour and attaching it to the person's identify.

Marge, Homer's long-suffering wife, cycles through the logical levels as she thinks:

ENVIRONMENT	'He has left his socks on the floor again.' (An environment observation)
BEHAVIOUR	'He will not pick up his socks.' (Describing his behaviour)
CAPABILITY	'He does not even know how to pick up his socks.' (He is not capable of picking up his socks.)
BELIEFS AND VALUES	'I don't think he cares.' He won't pick up his socks. (He expects someone else to do it for him.)
IDENTITY	'Who does he think he is?' He won't pick up his socks. ('He thinks he is too important/busy/different to pick up his socks.')

From Homer's point of view, he is thinking: 'What's up, Marge? You're moaning because I didn't pick up my socks. What's the big deal?' And he is genuinely perplexed.

Try it now: Recognizing 'flashpoints' using logical levels

1 Think back to the last time you said something you thought was trivial to someone and they responded with an 'over the top' reaction. Run through the situation in your mind again.

2 Is it possible that you were making a statement, and they were interpreting it from a different logical level?

3 Which of the logical levels might they have been reacting from?

4 What might you have done to calm down the situation?

When people are arguing on different levels of thinking, they are more likely to reach agreement if one person recognizes the level at which the other person is speaking, and then matches that level before attempting to calm the situation.

Try it now: Establish which logical level people are operating from

The next few times you watch people disagree on television news, dramas, in debates, or at home or in work, ignore the content of the argument and instead start to identify at which of the logical levels each person is operating from.

✳ Notice whether they are on the same level of thinking as each other.

✳ On which level are they talking from?

✳ On which level do you think the real issue belongs?

✳ Think about what sort of question you could ask that would have both parties discussing the matter on the same logical level.

Focus points

By the end of this chapter you will have:

* Learned if your inner team members are all routing for you
* Identified specific inner gremlins and their assigned tasks
* Selected your inner team cheerleaders – those with beliefs who support you
* 'Sent off' unhelpful team members to reduce the power of inner criticism
* Added some structure to your thinking using logical levels of thinking.

Next step

You have acquired a lot of skills now, and in the next chapter you will learn still more. There we will focus on whether you are extending yourself enough to attain your desires in life. You will also learn how to gather resources from what you have learned to create your own success.

8

Step to the edge of your boundaries

In this chapter you will:

▶ *Learn if you are extending yourself enough to attain your desires in life*

▶ *Gather resources from previous chapters to create your own success*

▶ *Change viewpoints for flexible thinking and to gather information*

▶ *Challenge limiting beliefs to create better alternative choices*

▶ *Use your learning tools to create a successful outcome.*

'Chains of habit are too light to be felt until they are too heavy to be broken.'

Warren Buffett, American business magnate

Case study: Tim Smit – turning dreams into reality

Tim Smit's vision created a garden called the Eden Project. On a wasteland site in Cornwall, England, with the help, energy and enthusiasm of those around him, the Dutch-born British businessman created one of the architectural wonders of our time. Tim admits he was a dreamer when he first conceived his idea of building the giant artificial biomes. Yet his dream has become a reality which more than one million people from all over the planet have come to visit.

The interesting thing about Smit is his total belief that the right people and situations would turn up at the right time. He also firmly believed that he could be the lynchpin that would be instrumental in building Eden. Yet if he had written a CV asking to be the architect of such an audacious plan, Smit would probably have been turned down because he did not fit the criteria for the job – he was a music producer.

'"Come to the edge," she said. They said, "We are afraid." "Come to the edge," she said. They came, she pushed them – they flew.'

Guillaume Apollinaire

Key idea: Are you extending yourself enough?

Often people don't extend themselves enough to 'live on the edge' and find out what else they might be capable of doing, outside their regular sphere of work. How many other potential Smits are there out there, serving customers, selling products, making their money in ordinary jobs?

Gather your resources to create your dream

If you want to succeed in life, you've got to create your own dream, with you in the starring role. You've got to believe in yourself and expect good things to happen.

Project a picture of yourself out into the world as a winner – see it, feel it, anticipate it until you can almost touch it. Then, expect to have good things projected back at you. None of us know what we are capable of achieving. It's only when we step to the edge of our boundaries and beyond that we begin to find our true potential.

Try it now: Examine your toolkit

Circle the tools you have acquired so far in this book, then list how you will use each one to project a good image of yourself, both internally to yourself and out into the world.

STRATEGY	RESOURCES	FLEXIBLE THINKING	INFORMATION GATHERING
Know how motivated you are on a scale of 1–10	Recognize your thinking patterns	Setting good outcomes – goal setting	See others' viewpoints
Use values to motivate yourself	Understand behaviour	Visualize best outcomes	Gather your resources
Model a skill for personal success	Notice sensory clues	Increase thinking skills; use other peoples' strategies	What tools do I have? What do I need?
Reframe limiting beliefs	Be at cause, not at the effect of others	Problem solving; chunk thinking up and down	Noticing what triggers you to get things done
Align beliefs and values	Anchoring – manage your internal state	Get into the right frame of mind	Use logical levels to view situations and gather information

In this chapter we will teach you how to identify and deal with limiting beliefs that may stop you reaching your potential goals. The aim is to let you try some techniques for countering self-doubt so that you see that these things work in the real world. Ultimately, however, you need to take personal responsibility for trying out, practising and incorporating the ideas that work best for you in your everyday life.

Once you have positively established the means, motive and opportunity ingredients described under goal setting in Chapter 3, it is your beliefs about yourself, your abilities and your motivation (Chapter 7) that will determine how successful you are. Your mission in this chapter, should you choose to accept it, is to bombard your brain with as much evidence as possible that you are a truly competent, confident and capable individual priming yourself like a heat-seeking missile guided towards its target.

Unshackle yourself from limiting beliefs

DON'T PUT OBSTACLES IN YOUR OWN WAY

Of all the things a person can say to themselves when faced with a difficult situation, 'I can't' is potentially the most limiting of all. When you hear someone utter the words 'I can't', you know that person is boxed-in or stuck in a way that that is currently cutting them off from finding a solution to their problem.

- ▶ 'I can't do it.'

- ▶ 'I can't get through it.'

- ▶ 'I can't see a way around it.'

IF YOU BELIEVE YOU HAVE A PROBLEM, THEN YOU HAVE ONE

If you believe you have a problem, then you do have one – whether it's real or not. If you watch the actions of someone telling you they cannot do something, often they will stretch their hands in front of them in a gesture of helplessness. They are in a state of confusion and are not thinking resourcefully. When someone else offers them a solution to their problem and they are in an 'I can't' frame of mind they are often likely to dismiss sound ideas as being unworkable or turn them down simply because they don't believe anything will work.

IN A CALMER STATE WE FIND SOLUTIONS

Once we're in a calmer and more resourceful state and we've found a solution, we inform people we've 'got over it', 'found a way round it' or, best of all, have 'sorted it out'. In this, more positive state we sift through the available information and look for recognizable patterns. We ask ourselves: 'Has this problem occurred before?', 'How was it tackled?', and 'What was the outcome?' We begin to come up with new stratagems for solving the problems.

Deletion, distortion and generalization

When we speak, we delete, distort and generalize incoming information depending on how we see and feel about others and what we think is going on in the world. If we feel bad about ourselves, we may treat ourselves harshly, so that when someone pays a compliment, instead of being pleased, we may be thinking: 'What do they want from me?'

If you questioned your habitual ways of thinking, how many of the everyday statements you make to yourself about situations would stand up to closer scrutiny? Below are a few common statements you may hear from others or think yourself, with questions to ask yourself in order to generate more information.

Deletions	Questions to elicit more information
'I'm not happy with this.'	What are you not happy about? In what way are you not happy?
'Nobody listens to what I'm saying.'	No one? Not one single person? Who, specifically, doesn't listen?
Cause and effect	**Questions to elicit more information**
'She makes me very angry.'	How does she make you angry? Has there ever been a time when she didn't make you angry?
Distortions	**Questions to elicit more information**
'All he does is criticize.'	Always? Without exception?
'She doesn't want me in her team.'	How do you know that?
'They think I'm useless.'	How do you know they think that?
Generalizations	**Questions to elicit more information**
'But, Mum, everybody does it.'	Who's everybody? What, every single person?
'Seminars are a waste of time.'	*All* seminars? Every single one?
Assumptions	**Questions to elicit more information**
'You don't buy me flowers – you don't love me anymore.'	'How does my not buying you flowers mean that I don't love you?'

If you find yourself thinking 'I can't do it!', ask yourself the questions, 'According to whom?', 'What is stopping you?'

Try it now: Changing 'I can't!' to 'I can't! do it yet!'

Relax, put your feet up, with a cup of tea and distance yourself. Think of a situation in the past where you made, or thought, one of these statements:

✳ 'I can't do it.'
✳ 'I can't get through it.'
✳ 'I can't see a way around it.'

Now think about the same situation and ask yourself what would happen if you applied a slightly different slant to your thoughts, for instance:

✳ 'I can't do it, yet!'
✳ 'I can't get through it, yet!'
✳ 'I can't see a way around it, yet! It will come.'

What adding the 'yet!' does is to give you some 'wriggle room'. It allows thinking time for a new way of seeing a solution to pop in. By contrast, 'I can't do it!' is like coming up against a brick wall – the statement simply stops you in your tracks.

The next time you feel blocked, apply the 'yet' to the end of your statement and then notice how new ideas for solutions start to bubble up and your ideas begin to change.

A powerful tool to confront negative beliefs

Gregg Levoy, journalist and motivational speaker, uses this wonderful written exercise for overcoming limiting beliefs in his 'Callings' Heart at Work workshops. For a negative belief that you hold – for example 'I can't write a bestseller', 'I can't set up my own business', 'I can't be the most successful salesman on the planet' – start questioning yourself about why you can't. Look on it as engaging in a conversation, or a dual between the negative and positive sides of your brain.

Allow Positive and Negative (you might want to call them Pat and Ned for short): one line for each statement. Start with a negative statement, then start the next line with a positive statement.

Each negative statement should comprise why you *can't* do something, and the following positive statement must comprise something that tells you why you *can*.

Example: 'I want to write a bestseller'

Ned: You can't write a bestseller.

Pat: How do you know that?

Ned: Well, you've never written one before.

Pat: That doesn't mean I couldn't.

Ned: Yes it does; you haven't got the discipline.

Pat: I have got discipline in other things, I could organize myself better.

Ned: You haven't got the talent, or the desire.

Pat: Yes I have, and I've always wanted to write a book.

Ned: When there's time, but you never have enough time.

Pat: I could make time…

Try it now: Challenge your negative beliefs about your abilities

Apply the negative-and-positive routine to one of your own limiting beliefs. It may be 'I can't do it because …' and then let the negative and positive team members inside you slog it out until you reach a natural winner and someone gives in.

Keep this going and don't stop until one side, either Pat or Ned, is exhausted and gives up because it has no more answers. Of more than 80 people at Greg Levoy's workshop who carried out this exercise, most were surprised that they successfully beat their negative 'I can't's' into submission. We are often afraid to argue with our negative beliefs because we are afraid of being proven wrong.

Experiment with this exercise a few times and see what sort of result you get. You may be pleasantly surprised. Another benefit of listing on paper your negative and positive thoughts about a subject is that you can spot whether your thinking becomes distorted.

AVOID 'ALL OR NOTHING' THINKING

Sometimes when we're working hard to reach a goal, things don't always go to plan. When you're tired and working hard to complete a project, it's easy to slip into 'all or nothing' thinking. But, if given free rein, negative thinking can fire off a chain of negative thoughts that will sabotage your efforts, and stop you breaking through your next boundary to success. If you catch yourself slipping into the 'I can't do this', 'I'll never finish', 'Why did I think I could do it?' vein of thought, which is designed to paralyse you with anxiety, depression or fear and make you less effective, then change your thinking immediately.

New projects can take a lot of initial effort and can sometimes be compared with a plane taking off. The plane requires its maximum capacity of fuel for the energy it needs to take off from the ground and become airborne. Once in flight, however, it cruises using only 37 per cent of the fuel it required for take-off. Don't assume that, because one thing failed, the whole project is a failure: it isn't.

If part of your plan doesn't work, keep your outcome in mind and try something different. Imagine a pilot who flies from the mainland to a small and difficult-to-get-to island off the coast. His flight is off course for 92 per cent of his flying time, but each time the pilot notices he corrects the flight path and the plane lands on schedule. This is often what happens when we make plans and set targets; we may have to change them a bit, but we still end up at the right destination.

Change your state / change your feelings

A person may work at a supermarket checkout counter where they behave in a restrained and predictable way, yet on Saturday night everything changes and they dress up and look fantastic. Before leaving home they engage in rituals to pamper themselves – they smell desirable, feel sexy and great, and run images of themselves being the best dancer on the floor. Guess what happens? They go out, enjoy themselves, get noticed; they get talked to and chatted up.

What happens on Monday morning back at the checkout? They change their state to behave in a way that is appropriate to their job situation.

What would happen if they decided that for just 20 minutes every morning they would go into 'disco chat-up and energy mode' as they served customers? They might get the sack; they might get noticed; they might get promoted; they might get customers enquiring about how they are. They might also start to become more flexible in their behaviour and realize that they can choose how they feel and act. We all have a choice about how we feel and act in any situation; we don't always have to go with the automatic response of the crowd.

Try it now: Behavioural experiment

1 Take one of the negative beliefs you hold about yourself and think about what a better, more helpful belief might be. (You might do this by saying: 'If I was fantastically clever and good at this thing, a better belief might be...')

2 Walk around for a day or so with this alternative belief about whatever it is you thought you couldn't do and notice what happens:
   ▷ What did you notice?
   ▷ What are you doing, or thinking, differently now that whatever you did before?

Our feelings are the most important things we possess. Our feelings dictate whether we are, say, happy, sad, unloved, hurt, welcome or outcast.

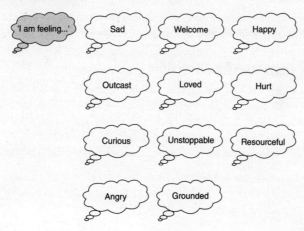

We may think that other people influence our feelings, but actually we can choose to manage our internal state and how we choose to feel. How often have you heard someone say, 'She makes me angry!' The truth is they don't make you angry; you *allow* yourself to feel angry about whatever that person said. By allowing your state, or how you feel, to be dictated to you by another person, you are giving up your power to someone else who can decide at a whim how they will 'make' you feel.

Remember this

As many as one-third of the population of some countries indulge in drug taking mainly because it changes the way they feel about themselves, how vividly and differently they see the world, and how happy, successful and loved they feel – sadly, for a short time only. Many crimes committed are drug related, and some addicts are prepared to swap their self-esteem, families, liberty and eventually their lives for tablets or a powder that lets them chase their 'feel good' state.

How you choose to feel and the state you choose to operate in can be within your control. I'm not saying it will be like getting high on drugs – it won't be so ruinous – but it can still feel pretty good. We all repeat patterns for the things we do, even those at which we are repeatedly unsuccessful.

Switching states – that is, creating an association between two experiences to create a strong mental state – is used a lot by sports and businesspeople, public speakers and musicians and others who need to give a consistently excellent performance.

Key idea: We can all change states at will

Most people can recall and associate with a sad experience or bad feelings at will. All it takes to trigger their mental movie is to say to them 'Remember when...' and they do the rest themselves. Their eyes will fix on a spot where they see the events happening, their shoulders will crumple, their breathing will slow down as they relive again the emotions they felt that first time.

So why not choose a ritual that is linked to success? Use it as a trigger to recall a time when you felt truly alive and powerful, when everything you did seemed like magic.

Try it now: Never miss an opportunity to anchor good feelings

1 Think of a situation in which you may need to influence others. It may be when giving a presentation, talking to colleagues, or asking for a favour or for something that you might not necessarily get, for example a contract.

2 Now think of an activity that you enjoy doing about which you feel confident and proficient. Run your mental movie and associate with the images and become part of them. As you run through them in your happy state, feel your emotions intensify and become stronger. As the colours in the pictures become bigger, brighter, bolder and closer, just sigh and let all the good feelings wash over you.

3 Now shake off that image and put it aside for a moment. Think about how giving your presentation, for example, will be easier once you transfer your confident and happy, relaxed feelings from your more empowering state.

4 This time, as you see yourself watching an internal movie of you giving your talk or presentation, notice that you have distanced yourself and are not in the picture – in fact, you are actually watching the movie from outside. Now, from this distant back-row view, you can observe in a detached way more about what is happening.

5 Run your 'feel good' movie again to the point where you feel most powerful, confident and alive. As your feelings become stronger, touch your thumb and forefinger together as an emotional trigger and feel yourself leap, taking those strong, feeling good emotions into your less colourful movie.

6 Bring all the good feelings associated with your 'feel good' movie into a second movie in which you want to experience having a really successful outcome. You're no longer watching a drab or uncomfortable movie; you're actually in it. But you've brought all the strength, determination and confidence with you from your most empowering feelings and images.

7 Remember the strong feelings you had when you pressed your thumb and forefinger together when you changed your mental movie? You can use that action to anchor your good feelings in the future. With a little practice you will be able to recall and trigger this powerful emotional state just by pressing your thumb and forefinger together.

Changing viewpoints

'Before you can know how another man thinks, you must walk a mile in his moccasins.'

Native American saying

If you are running negative thinking loops, you might be too close to the situation you're dealing with to get a rational perspective on what is going on. At times like this it's often good to stand back and distance yourself from the situation for a while – even just making yourself a cup of tea can help put the situation into perspective.

Adopting different perceptual positions can be used:

▶ to imagine how your behaviour may be impacting on others

▶ to think about how your behaviour might be viewed by an objective, dispassionate outsider

▶ to notice what you are feeling inside about a situation

▶ to imagine what it feels like to be another person.

If you have not found a solution to your problem using other means, then try adopting different viewpoints and ask yourself questions about the situation. This will give you more valuable information about the situation than you could ever have gained by observing it from only one point of view.

Try it now: Increase your flexible thinking

Practise switching your perspectives on a situation at will. Imagine you are a character from a TV programme, an 'outsider' like the Vulcan scientist Spock of the Starship *Enterprise*. How would he view what was going on if he were watching you in one of your difficult encounters with other people?

Remember this: We already change viewpoints

We adopt different perceptual positions constantly. Sometimes we feel involved and get close up and personal – we feel strong emotions about what is going on. At other times we can distance ourselves from events and this helps us to think more objectively. Each type of observation gives us different types of information about the situation or issue.

Focus points

By the end of this chapter you will have:

✳ Learned if you are extending yourself enough to attain your goals in life
✳ Gathered resources from previous chapters to create your own success
✳ Challenged limiting beliefs to create better alternative choices
✳ Changed viewpoints for flexible thinking and to gather information
✳ Used your learning tools to create a successful outcome.

Next step

There is a saying that, if the only tool you have is a hammer, then the solution to every problem will be a nail. Now that you have amassed a powerful toolkit that you can use for problem solving and overcoming limiting beliefs, weigh up each technique and think about how useful it might be and in what kinds of circumstance. When you execute a problem-solving technique notice what changes, how it changes, and whether your result was the one you wanted. The better you understand someone's thinking strategies, the more able you are to influence and predict their behaviour, which is the subject that we will cover in the next chapter. You have the power to take personal responsibility for motivating yourself to make things happen – so use it.

9

Understand people's thinking styles

In this chapter you will:

▶ *Learn how to notice how people make decisions based on what they see, hear and feel*

▶ *Learn how to recognize people's different types of thinking style*

▶ *Discover how to identify your own thinking habits, triggers and motivational drives*

▶ *Understand how thinking styles builds rapport and communication with others*

▶ *Learn how to communicate with a group to get your message across.*

Notice how people make decisions

> 'The most complicated piece of equipment comes with no instructions and performs in a different way every day – it's our people.'
>
> Sir Tom Farmer, CEO Kwik-Fit

One of the most useful skills you can develop is to notice how people make their decisions. It may be the steps leading to them buying a new product, changing their job, electing a new president or choosing a restaurant meal. If you can identify people's thinking and behaviour patterns in advance, you can determine or influence how they make their choices in the future.

The following is adapted from an article I wrote for the 'NLP Expert Column' of *Positive Health* magazine 'Recognising Thinking Styles', issue 207, June 2013, www.positivehealth. com/author/frances-coombes/frances-coombes

---

The next time you go for a meal ask at least six people how they chose their last restaurant meal and record their answers.

ANALYSE THE PROCESS: Ask each person what is the first sensation they are aware of as they start to think about food and make their choice. — What was their process of choosing? Get them to take you through the steps up to the point where they make their decision. (You will find that naturally slim people will have a different selection style to people who are chubbier.)

NOTICE SENSORY LANGUAGE: Did they get a feeling first that told them they were hungry? Did they see the food in their mind's eye? Did they talk to themselves and run through each dish in turn, imagining tasting it. Build up a whole sensory sequence for how they made their choice. — Was their language mainly: visual (describing what they were seeing); auditory (describing what they were saying to themselves); kinaesthetic (giving a sense of how they were feeling about the experience)?

IDENTIFY THE TRIGGER: Where did their trigger begin? Was it with a feeling? A smell? A taste? A picture? Something they said to themselves before taking the actions? — What was their trigger point: how did they flip from indecision to having made up their mind?

How might this information be useful to you?

If you were devising a slimming programme to suit your habits, you might want to try on some of the thinking strategies for choosing a meal that slim people run around food, and see which ones you prefer that would work for you.

Naturally slim people's strategies

Theresa: 'I think: what have I eaten last night, and what will I eat tomorrow, and what would be a good choice that would let me try something different from either?'

Ruth: 'I pat my stomach and think: how full do I feel now? And how do I want to feel after I have eaten this meal? And what would be a good choice to give me that feeling?'

Other strategies for choosing a meal

Friends who are not so slim will run other types of strategies for choosing.

Carole: 'I read each dish on the menu and imagine tasting each one in turn. Then I narrow it down to three choices and then decide what I am going to have.'

Ben: 'I look at the menu, then ask what everyone else is having, and then choose what I think someone else who has made a good choice chooses.'

People tend to run patterns of behaviours in similar situations. If you know how they behave in one situation, you can predict how they are likely to behave in a similar situation in the future.

Try it now: Notice restaurants and what sort of sensory eaters they attract

When you're out, start to notice restaurants, and decide which type of customer they might attract? For instance, some Chinese restaurants simply have large pictures of what their main dishes look like. What type of customer are they attracting? Some eating places have smells of coffee, warm bread or food pumping out. Some restaurants will have menus outside which exquisitely describe the mouth-watering experience of tasting the food. What kind of person are they attracting? Which predominately sensory types (visual/auditory/gustatory/olfactory/kinaesthetic)?

Noticing thinking styles

Key idea: What are thinking styles?

* Thinking styles are mainly unconscious patterns of thinking we use to sort out all the incoming information that we are bombarded with each day. Our thinking patterns affect what we notice about a situation, how we visualize it, and how we organize and structure it in order to come to a conclusion.

* The connections we make and the way we view the world, our memories, ideas and incoming information are all unique to us. We take in information from the world through all our senses – that is, what we are see, hear, touch, taste and smell.

* If we did not have an internal system which filtered information for us, we would be overwhelmed by thousands of unwanted stimuli such as newspaper headlines, snippets of conversations, snippets of songs, labels on food product, etc. Our thinking patterns screen out what does not interest us, so we can pay more attention to the things we are drawn to.

Why do people behave so differently from each other? You ask several people to do the same thing, so why is it that one does exactly what you say; another wants to discuss it and finds fault, or argues with you on each point; while a third person may completely ignore your request?

Different people run different thinking styles!

When we recognize the styles that people are running, we are able to make requests in ways that make it more likely that things will get done, because the requests can be addressed to people in ways that meet their needs.

Case study: Fiona Beddoes-Jones's 'Thinking Styles'

According to Fiona Beddoes-Jones, management consultant and creator of the training programme 'Thinking Styles', 'People who don't notice the small, to them unimportant, things may be "big chunk thinkers", interested in what we are going to do, not the minutiae of how we are going to get there. They might be people with a poorly developed mental filing system. Or they could be "mismatchers" – people who hate being told what to do.' As part of her programme, Fiona has developed a questionnaire that teaches staff first how to understand their own thinking style, then to apply it to other people's styles so they can learn to work together effectively as a team.

Some people, Fiona points out, are visual and see pictures when they think. But if you are an auditory person and hear what people say, it may not occur to you that others take in information differently. Fiona suggests: 'Shut your eyes and listen to the words people use to engage with each other in your department. Someone who says "I see what you mean" is thinking in pictures. To talk to them in their own language and find out if they understand your message, you might say "Do you get the picture?"' Other people are predominately intuitive. You can recognize their speech because they use phrases like 'I feel we should do this'. You will get more detailed information back from them if you ask how they 'feel' about it.

People also have styles of working with others. 'Matchers' are team people who like to work in harmony. They are good communicators and do well in customer relations jobs. Matchers are adaptive and tend to fit in with other people's wishes. They are not normally innovators, simply because they are too nice. Mismatchers, by contrast, think ideas through by disagreement

'The first time you talk an idea through with a mismatcher,' says Fiona, 'they usually disagree with you. But when you return they will have thought about it and be working towards an agreement. Mismatchers make good computer hardware engineers because they will be acutely aware of all possible risks involved.'

We all use combinations of different thinking styles that can change depending on the task we are working on, how relaxed or stressed we feel and where we happen to be. The best type of thinker to be is a flexible one.

Shell and National Westminster Bank have used 'Thinking Styles' to match jobs to the way people naturally process information. British Aerospace used it to allocate tasks among teams of workers. Fiona says, 'When projects cost millions, anything that leads to team effectiveness and shortens the length of a job can potentially save huge amounts of money.'

DO YOU RECOGNIZE YOUR THINKING STYLE?

It is best to think of thinking types as being tendencies on a number of different scales, or continuums:

▶ Moving away from ← → Moving towards

People who move away from pain may be spurred into action to avoid unpleasant situations or when things become unbearable. When you ask people what they want and they tell you what they do not want, you will know they are running an 'away from' style of thinking. To motivate someone who runs an 'away from pain' thinking style, tell them about all the unpleasant things that will happen if they do not reach their target.

When people tell you what they want, and what they want to accomplish, their thinking strategy is to move towards pleasure. Show them the carrot and the rewards they will get for their effort.

▶ Necessity ← → Possibility

Some people are driven by what *must* be done, or what they think *should* be done. 'I must do this' is their mantra. People who are driven by necessity will often have a preference for procedures and have strong ideas about how things should be done.

People who are motivated by what could be want options and new ventures and novel ways to do things. They like to know what the alternatives are and what might be possible.

▶ Focus attention on themselves ← → Focus on others

People who are self-referenced evaluate a situation from their own perspective and may not always consider effects on others. At the extreme they may be oblivious to the outside world and how situations are being experienced by other people. Extremely self-referenced behaviour may be seen as selfish or narcissistic.

Those who focus on others and how situations will affect them are often carers and may put the contentment and welfare of others over their own needs. They are attentive to what is going on around them and, at the extreme, may end up trying to please everyone at their own expense.

▶ Sort for similarities ← → Look for differences

People who sort for similarities notice what is similar in a situation to what has gone before. The want stability and to find common ground with others. They quickest way to get a result from them is to build rapport with them.

Those who filter for differences may notice what has changed or is different from before. They make good colleagues to have in a crisis-management situation because they pick up on every eventuality and possibility that might go wrong. They are good people to have on your team for spotting errors, but not to live with.

▶ Big chunk thinker ← → Small chunk thinker

Big-chunk thinkers are able to assess a whole situation. They take in larger pieces of information and key points. Big chunk thinkers are often leaders or responsible for major projects. They may be more concerned with the big picture rather than the fine details of how they plan to get there.

Small chunk thinkers are often procedural thinkers. They follow instructions and the accepted way of doing things. If you interrupt extremely procedural thinkers while they are talking, they may need to go back and recount the whole story from the beginning again.

Remember this

People use combinations of lots of different thinking styles but they do have traits. Some types of thinker are easy to recognize because they operate at the extreme ends of their scale.

THE ADVANTAGES OF RECOGNIZING THINKING STYLES

▶ When you know how you think, you understand how you function and you can organize the things you want to do in ways that are most likely to lead to you achieving your outcomes.

▶ By learning to manage our thoughts we can shape them and change them so that we can create the life and career we want.

- You can organize your time more effectively because you understand how you think and behave and get things done.

- You can build your own personal profile of your thinking habits in order to understand why you do the things you do.

- You can choose a career that is attractive to someone with your thinking pattern.

- Understanding more about thinking styles can help us understand more about other people.

- You can select staff that fit particular jobs, based on knowing how they think.

- If you are aware of someone's thinking style, it is easier to negotiate with them or influence them.

Remember this

* Although people display patterns of behaviour which you can observe and sometimes predict, it does not mean that they will behave in the same way all the time. In fact, most of us have a capacity to surprise others.
* Flexible thinkers can change their habitual thinking style at will and can operate well in other styles, too. For instance, a project manager may be a big chunk thinker, and able to visualize and have an overview of a major plan, say to build a hospital. He will also, however, be good at breaking down the steps required for the outcome into procedural bite-sized chunks.

Try it now: What type of thinker are you?

1 Go back the discussion of thinking styles above and decide which best describes you.
2 Mark yourself on a scale of 1–10 on how strongly ingrained you feel each behaviour is in you.
3 What have you learned about yourself and your thinking styles that you did not know before?
4 Are there any thinking behaviours that you might like to change?
5 Visualize what would be the outcome if you changed a thinking behaviour?

Communicating and building rapport

People have preferential sensory systems for the way they take in information from the world. You can build rapport with them by speaking the same sensory language as they do. Using the same representation system as people builds rapport, while interrupting using another system will break rapport. It's good to know how to nurture rapport, but it's also good to know how to break it if you want to move a conversation along.

Remember this: Communicate in people's language

If you tell people your message in their preferred sensory style, they will learn and retain it better than if it is given in another style.

Studies carried out with children and adults, looking at how they learn and take in information, suggest that there are four main learning styles:

▶ **Visual (pictures)** People who use predominantly visual senses are good at sorting lots of information at a moment's notice. They may think in pictures and hold and rearrange information in a spider diagram.

▶ **Auditory (words)** People who think in words find it difficult to hold information unless it is structured and the relationship is linear. They often use chants and mnemonics to help them remember things. The auditory style is good for sorting known information, but is less useful for being creative.

▶ **Kinaesthetic (tactile)** People whose dominant sense is touch may need to physically do an exercise a couple of times before they can master it. We retain a lot of information in our body. If you have not ridden a bike for a long while and you sit on one, your body knows how to ride a bike even if you cannot consciously remember.

▶ **Emotions** People who process through feelings, sensations and emotions are often very bright but may never have learned to process that information in a way that can be checked by others. Once triggered, this system will produce a mass of information at once, leading to a 'flash' of understanding.

Below are some reasons why it's invaluable to know other people's thinking styles when you communicate with them:

▶ If you are a leader and need to motivate others, then knowing how your people take in information and think will help you to communicate more effectively with them.

▶ When you know how your own internal motivation works, you can more easily understand other people's patterns and the best ways to guide and motivate them.

▶ If you understand more about the way people think, you can build rapport and have stronger relationships with clients, colleagues and friends and on a deeper level than before.

▶ You can speak to groups of people using words that appeal to a range of thinking styles.

▶ You will become more capable of generating favourable or win–win solutions. If you can see more sides to a disagreement or problem, you are likely also to see more possibilities for solving it.

▶ If you are writing job adverts or advertising brochures and you want to appeal to a specific kind of reader, you can write in language that appeals to the thinking styles you seek in an applicant.

Connect with your audience when giving a presentation

When giving a presentation, your audience expects you to fulfil their expectations. They want you to provide linked information, tell stories and jokes, and give hand-outs and exercises that will make your talk memorable. If you present your message so that it is appealing to several types of listener, you can ensure that everyone in your audience connects with and remembers what you said.

It can be useful here to think of the way products are communicated in the world of advertising. A lot of advertising is aimed at people who run an 'away from pain' strategy. The messages about the penalties of not buying the right car insurance or not having the right Internet search engine is that, if you do not do these things, it will cause you pain. Yet that message may be largely ignored by the part of the population not hung up on the 'feel bad' factor. If the message is not packaged in a way that fits their criteria, those people will simply switch off and not notice it.

If you are presenting to a general audience and you don't know their background, then consider this:

▶ The biggest part of the population, 35 per cent, want to know *why* they should listen to you. So you have to win their hearts and minds and tell them at the start why what you have to say is important to them.

▶ One-quarter, 25 per cent, of your audience are thinking 'So what?' They want to know *how useful* whatever you are saying to them is.

▶ Just under one-quarter of your audience, 22 per cent, are wondering, 'How do *apply* I this information? Show me how to use it.'

▶ And the remainder, 18 per cent, of the group are thinking 'What if…?' What if I took this information and customized it? What does it mean to me and what can I do with it? What might it lead to? (The statistics are from Bernice McCarthy's 4MAT System.)

If you are speaking to a group and you want to influence people, look through your notes to see whether your presentation will satisfy the sort of questions that a general audience would want answered.

Try this: Tip for connecting with your target audience

When preparing a presentation, cut out magazine pictures of people who represent your typical audience. Stick them on the wall and glance up at them as you write. If you give each person in your pictures a name and then write the words 'Why?', 'What?', 'So what?' and 'How?' under each one, you can converse with each part of your audience individually at any brief sticking point. You can simply stop and say to 'So what?' – 'Well, Dave, what did you think of the way I put that?' – and wait for the answer.

Focus points

By the end of this chapter you will have:

* Noticed how people make decisions based on what they see, hear, feel
* Recognized people's different thinking styles
* Identified your own thinking habits, triggers and motivational drives
* Built rapport and communication with others using your knowledge of thinking styles
* Learned how to communicate with a group to get your message across.

Next step

If you are going to take somebody to a new level of understanding, you have to get there first yourself. In order to convey information to a group of people, your energy level, state, motivation and enthusiasm must be higher than your audience's. It is your internal state and level of motivation that determine how well your talk will go.

In the next chapter we will go more deeply into thinking styles, especially with regard to the world of sales.

10

Take control of how you think

In this chapter you will:

▶ *Notice behaviour: how do people become motivated to buy?*

▶ *Take a snapshot of your thinking habits: create a blueprint of how you think*

▶ *Learn the three parts to changing beliefs*

▶ *Notice your triggers and how you become motivated to make decisions*

▶ *Look at what is holding a habit in place and thus how to change it*

▶ *Get curious about people's thinking styles.*

How do people become motivated to buy something new?

The Canadian Shelle Rose Charvet is an international communications and influencing skills trainer and the author of *Words That Change Minds* (Kendall Hunt Publications, 1997). She has trained sales groups in large companies in how to get the edge in selling, and has helped Canadian political parties design campaigning strategies based on understanding how differently people think and make decisions (such as who they are going to vote for).

Charvet says, 'The better you understand someone's thinking strategies, the more able you are to influence and predict their behaviour. Whether you are a team leader, a parent, a colleague, or a lover, you need to know which of your people are motivated by external circumstances, that is praise, rewards, recognition, and which are motivated by their internal beliefs and values.'

If you are selling your product or idea to someone, the better you understand how people think and comprehend their internal drivers, the more able you are to influence and predict their behaviour:

▸ There are people who move 'away from pain' and at the other end of the scale those who are motivated to move 'towards pleasure'.

▸ Some customers want a new product to be 'different' and others look for 'sameness' to whatever they are using now.

▸ There are also 'sameness with exception' people who like to know the product is similar to the one they had before and then to hear words such as 'improvement', 'better', 'more' or 'less'.

Everyone has different triggers, so start to notice yours.

Case study: Buying an iPod

In a recent training session I ran, several people were in the process of buying iPods. We explored their triggers, that final thought that pushes them over the edge, to finally make the purchase.

Dennis

Dennis needed to know everything about the product, and to do comparisons with every other product available. He needed to know that whatever he bought was the best. He had a strong perfectionist streak in him and could not bear the thought of having purchased something and then finding out there was a better deal on the market.

The trigger for being satisfied was that, once he had done his homework, he needed an expert. Someone with authority whom he trusted to say, 'This is the best deal you can get.' Dennis, then, trusted his own opinion but also needed to seek outside verification as the trigger for buying.

Noel

Noel had been looping through thinking circles for weeks. He had done all his homework, had even been to the store to try the products out and still hadn't bought the iPod. He had all the information he needed and was becoming intensely frustrated because he had frittered away so much time deciding on his choice, and yet still he waited.

So we asked Noel, 'What extra piece of information would you require in order to make the purchase?' Noel realized that when all his other criteria were satisfied, the final trigger was that he had to know he was getting a good deal. There had to be some kind of bargain attached to the deal.

He returned the following week, with his iPod, and told us he had gone into the store to look, seen the product he liked, and been told that there was a special deal. He bought it on the spot and was delighted with his purchase.

Faye

Faye was motivated differently from the others. She decided she needed an iPod, looked around to see who else had one, and played with a friend's product. She liked the feel and experience of holding it, went to the store and bought one just like it the following day.

Faye's criteria for buying were:
1 She had to feel she needed the goods.
2 She sought recommendations from a friend.

3 She had to physically touch and hold the product and play with it. If all was well, she would go to the shop and buy it.

Noel admitted that at first he had thought Faye's strategy reckless; then he was 'blown away' with it. He realized that Faye had spent only an hour or two on the whole process from research to purchase, and she was just as delighted with her purchase as he was. Noel said: 'With my buying strategy I have been clogging up my mind for weeks and becoming more and more frustrated.' He had tried using Faye's strategy for making decisions about other things and felt amazed and delighted that he had got so much more done.

People who are perfectionists may procrastinate well beyond what seems a necessary timespan because they are afraid of making a wrong decision. We asked Faye: 'What would happen if you made a wrong choice and your product turned out not to be the best one?' She replied: 'I would live with it! I made my decision, I tried the product before buying, I felt happy with my choice. If something else comes along that's better, it makes no difference to me because I already made my choice and am happy with that.'

Sometimes people who feel unconfident about a decision will perform the same thinking procedures over and over again before they finally take an action. Once people recognize the unproductive energy-sapping behaviour they are indulging in, they can often change their habits within a few minutes by practising and removing the 'looped thinking'.

The trigger to get them to change their unproductive thinking and behaviour patterns is often to say to them: 'Now, what are you going to do with all that extra time you will be freeing up in your life now you are not indulging in this behaviour?' This, I believe, really motivates people to keep the new, less stressful, more time-saving behaviour going.

Remember this: You can remove looped thinking

Identify parts of your behaviour that are not useful, and remove looped thinking patterns. This will enable you to take actions that produce results you want much more quickly than before.

Try it now: How do *you* become motivated to buy something new?

1 Think back to the last three times you bought something new, something that was important to you so you had to think about it a bit and compare it with other products. Now write down, or think through, how you made your choice.
  ▷ If it was a new computer, or an iPod, did you want it because the previous one broke down. Or did you see something better and say 'Oh wow! I want that.' What was your internal driver?
  ▷ Did you run away from pain or towards pleasure? Where are you on the continuum below? Put an X where you think you are when choosing a new product that's important to you.
  Away from pain ◀──────────────▶ *Towards pleasure*
2 Some customers want a new product to be 'different' and others look for 'sameness' to whatever they are using now. Did you choose it because it was similar to what you already had? Or did you want something completely different?
  Looks for sameness ◀──────────────▶ *Looks for difference*
3 There are also 'sameness with exception' people who like to know the product is similar to the one they had before and then to hear words such as 'improvement', 'better', 'more', 'less'.
  Sameness with improvements ◀──────────────▶ *Go-faster stripes*

Shelle Rose Charvet says: 'It's not just individuals; professions also have "towards" or "away from" attitudes. If you're addressing salespeople, they tend to move towards goals. While doctors move away from sickness and prefer speakers who take a similar cautious approach.' She continues: 'Can you imagine rushing in to see your doctor about a medical condition to be greeted by a cheerful "towards" person who ignores your symptoms and instead asks you, "What are your health goals?"'

Knowing your own internal drivers, and how you become motivated to buy a new product, how would you sell your next product or idea to someone who thought just like you? What are the sentences you could utter that would push their internal 'hot' buttons? What could you achieve if you recognized everyone's mechanism for becoming motivated? How much easier might it be for you to put your ideas across, get them heard and accepted?

Try it now: Notice other people's triggers and what motivates them to make changes

Choose a minimum of three different people to ask these questions, so that you can experience different thinking styles in action. Note what they say about how they made their choice and what the trigger point was that made them take the action.

You can find out what motivates a person by asking them a question such as:
✱ 'Why did you decide to change your last job?'
✱ 'Why did you change your last partner?'
Choose a question where they can tell you *why* they changed something.

People who move towards pleasure will tell you, 'Well, I saw this great job. It offered a lot of potential for me to do the sort of things I wanted,' and they will offer a list of criteria. People who move away from pain will say, 'Well, I couldn't stand my job anymore, and so I left.'

When it comes to partners the story is similar. People who move away from pain will say, 'Well, I couldn't stand it anymore so I got out.' The person who is motivated towards a goal might say, 'Well, I found a better partner, so I grabbed the chance to be happy.'

Remember this: People become motivated in different ways

Don't assume that people who run an 'away from' pain strategy will do any less well than those who 'move towards' fulfilment. Both types can be phenomenally successful but are motivated towards their goals in different ways.

Case study: George Soros

George Soros, the man who 'broke the bank of England' and made billions of pounds on the stock market, was in early life motivated by an 'away from pain' strategy. He recounts being completely broke. 'I have touched bottom,' he told himself, 'and I am bound to rise. This will be a valuable experience.' He was anxious never to touch bottom again. Memories that pressed Soros's 'hot' buttons and spurred his internal drivers towards unimaginable financial wealth were initially those of getting away from poverty and lack.

A thinking style checklist

As we saw in Chapter 9, there are recognizable thinking styles that people run in similar contexts. These methods of organizing information are patterns of thinking and behaviour that are outside our awareness, yet they have a major effect on how we respond to situations in the world. Knowing how habitual thinking patterns work will give you a better understanding of how you are motivated. This is useful information for:

▶ when you are setting your goals

▶ knowing other people's thinking styles

▶ building rapport with others.

Understanding thinking styles allows you to plan ahead how you might interact with other people, and alter your behaviour to get the best results from others and the outcomes you desire. The list below shows the characteristic behaviour of people who fall within each of the two broad thinking styles, 'away from pain' and 'towards pleasure':

People who move away from pain...

▶ focus on problems

▶ talk about what they do not want to happen

▶ often have difficulty defining their goals.

▶ are motivated by negative consequences

People who move towards pleasure...

▶ respond to incentives

▶ may find it difficult to recognize negative consequences.

▶ are motivated by achievements

People motivated by necessity

▶ often display driven behaviour

▶ are motivated by clear-cut, recognizable methods.

▶ have strong ideas on how things should be done

People motivated by options and possibility...

- want choices and lots of options
- are motivated by new challenges.
- are good at thinking up new ways of doing things

People who are internally focused...

- respond to the content of the communication
- do not easily build rapport with others.
- do not notice or respond to others' emotional behaviour

People whose attention is focused on others...

- respond to the people around them
- take responsibility for the way that other people feel.
- are good rapport builders

People who sort for similarities...

- will notice what is the same in a situation
- use words like 'just like me', 'the same', 'similar'.
- will often repeat a story similar to the one you tell

People who sort for what is different...

- notice what is different
- can be fault–finders.
- sort for what is missing

Big chunk thinkers...

- take a global view of an idea or situation
- can overlook things that do not fit into an overall plan.
- do not pay attention to the small details

Small chunk thinkers...

- are good at remembering and handling details
- like to be familiar with the process of doing things.
- may lack an overall framework to relate an idea to

You undertook a similar exercise to the one below in Chapter 9. However, it will be useful for you to assess your own thinking style(s) again, as your reflections are likely to have modified and deepened your ideas.

Try it now: Identify your thinking patterns to know how you become motivated

Look at the checklist of thinking styles descriptions above and mentally replay some recent situations in your head and how you reacted at the time. Ask yourself which type of thinking you habitually use – that is, your thinking style.

Check where you are on the continuum using the thinking style continuums below. Draw an X on the line at the point where you think you function in that particular thinking style.

1 *Away from pain* ◄──────────────► *Towards pleasure*
2 *Necessity* ◄──────────────────► *Possibility*
3 *Self-referenced* ◄────────────► *Respond to others*
4 *Sort for similarities* ◄───────► *Look for difference*
5 *Big picture thinker* ◄─────────► *Small chunk thinker*

What you have now is a blueprint of your thinking style, indicating your most dominant drivers and behaviour patterns. A mixture of these thinking habits, beliefs and behaviours will form the basis of how you become motivated to achieve your outcomes and, if you are that way inclined, reach your heart's desires in life.

Remember this

Thinking styles are useful predictors of behaviour, and recognizing and understanding them allows you to make crucial distinctions about how to interact with people. They are guides to behaviour only – no one is exclusively programmed to behave in a certain way. And we can all, with practice, learn to change unhelpful or irritating behaviour.

Where do your decisions come from?

How do you make decisions? Internally referenced people gather information from outside sources and then make a decision about it, based on their internal standards. External people need other people's opinions to help them make up their mind. It's vital to know how you make decisions because it will determine the way in which you are motivated.

Key idea

You can find out how people make decisions by asking them, 'How do you know when you have done a good job?' Ask this question of a good number of people, say the next six people you meet, so that you get a selection of answers:

* Some people will say: 'Oh, I just know when I've done a good job. It's a feeling.' These people are internally referenced and look inside themselves for the answers.
* Others will say, 'I know I've done well when my supervisor/friends/colleagues tell me I've done well.' These people are externally referenced and they seek confirmation from people outside.
* Some people will say, 'Well, I suppose that it's me who really knows when I've done something well. But I like somebody to tell me so, too.'

Try it now: How do *you* know when you have done a good job?

Which of the methods above do you use to know whether you have done a good job? Or do you have a different method? Write it down.

What have you learned about yourself and how you know that you have done a good job that you did not know before? Write or articulate out loud as if you were telling someone else how you know you have done a good job.

The distinction can have important implications for the success of internal communications within a company. Shelle observes: 'Whenever I am called into a large corporation and I keep hearing similar statements from employees – "The bosses keep us in the dark and don't tell us anything" – I can predict that I am dealing with an organization whose managers are mostly internally focused, and a workforce who are predominantly externally referenced and need to be told they have done a good job.'

Because the managers don't need someone else's approval on how well they think they are doing, they can't see what the problem is for the staff and why they need to be constantly updated.

Thinking styles also influence the way people react when confronted with problems:

▶ 'It's here so let's deal with it.' (*Towards resolution*)

▶ 'Oh no, not again. Let's ignore it and see if it goes away.' (*Away from pain*)

These are extremes on the continuum scale of reactions, but are pretty much how people think. People tend to run patterns of behaviour in similar circumstances. Although you can often predict how they will behave in one situation, this does not necessarily mean they will run the same behaviour in another context.

Remember this

✳ Understanding other people's behaviour will let you know what really motivates and triggers them to perform at their best.

✳ Understanding your own habitual behaviour lets you realize that there are choices you can make, that you don't have to be stuck, and that there are a variety of different ways of doing things.

Take control of how you think

The way you brush your teeth, use your knife and fork, choose the hand to drink your cup of tea with, are all habits you've formed. Try brushing your teeth with the other hand and see how different it feels initially. Most of us also think in habitual ways, and there is a multibillion pound global industry engaged in finding out about how we think in order to get us to buy into ideas, beliefs and products.

Our thinking habits are so deeply ingrained that, when we are stressed, they can resurface. Stressed people often reconnect to feelings of panic and dread experienced in childhood. It may be 20 years later and the person is a successful executive, but when faced with a deadline or a bigger challenge the old feelings of panic re-emerge. It's just as if they are handing in that classroom essay again and are expecting to receive bad marks!

All is not lost, however. With practice you can control your thinking styles and habits so that they do not ambush you unawares. First, however, you need to take a snapshot of your thinking habits when faced with a problem. Then you can create a blueprint for how to overcoming blocks to your success.

Try it now: Take a snapshot of your thinking habits

1 Can you remember the last problem you had that you successfully solved? Reflect on the following questions:
  ▷ How did you experience the problem?
  ▷ What were you see, hearing, feeling, about the situation?
  ▷ What was stopping you from moving ahead?
  ▷ What was the trigger that helped you move forward?
  What have you learned that you can take away and use?

2 Next 'measure' your thinking habits. Jot down your thoughts and feelings about your last challenge sequentially, paying attention to feelings from just before you realized there was a problem until just after you realized it was resolved. What were you saying to yourself?
  ▷ **Away from pain vs. Towards pleasure** Did I see this problem coming but put it off until it could no longer be avoided? Or did I see the possibilities in the situation and move towards making changes?
  ▷ **Necessity vs. Possibility** Is this a problem because I think it is, or because someone else has told me it is?
  ▷ **Self-referenced vs. Respond to others** Am I worried about the consequences for myself, for other people or both?
  ▷ **Sort of similarities vs. Look for difference** Is this problem similar to or different from other problems I've faced before? If so, how is it similar/different?
  ▷ **Big picture thinker vs. small chunk thinker** If you are thinking 'This always happens to me', you are generalizing. Asking yourself why this specific thing is happening is a more useful question that will generate more answers.

Try it now: Creating a blueprint for overcoming blocks to success

Think back to at least three previous situations where you thought you could not do something, and then changed your mind and decided you could. Now think about what happened to make you change your mind and decide that you could reach your goal.

1 What changed in the 'sights' and 'sounds' and 'feelings' you were experiencing to help you achieve your outcome? Highlight those sensations and write down what happened.

  ▷ What were you seeing, what were you saying to yourself, what were you hearing other people say that triggered your hot buttons and spurred you on to make the change? What were you feeling? Did a heat flush up inside you? Or did the hairs rise up on your neck or arms? Did a warm feeling flush up inside you? If so, where in your body did it start?

  ▷ Did you suddenly have the answer in a flash, or did it gradually creep up on you?

2 Write your procedure down so that the next time you feel blocked you can refer to it and remember how you made changes in your thinking in the past. Use it as a tool or resource to spur you on whenever you are blocked.

Once you understand your own behaviour patterns when faced with problems and how you solved them in the past, you can record this information and let it work for you, using it to bust unhelpful blocked thinking and propel you more quickly towards your goals.

Let's look more closely at how you can change your beliefs, exchanging negative for positive ones.

CHANGING BELIEFS

Gill Shaw, NLP executive and brand coach of Fresh-look Experience, says, 'Beliefs are our driving principles which give us a sense of certainty, realism and direction, particularly in decision making. Positive beliefs are necessary to achieve our outcomes, and may even become our purpose. Beliefs work in conjunction with our values, which are the standards which frame how we live and provide the juice to motivate us.'

There are three parts to changing beliefs:

1 **It's possible.** To be able to change a negative belief to a positive one, you need to reframe it and believe that it is possible to achieve (so that you can model success).

2 **You are able to do it.** You are able to achieve your goal with the resources you have available, and you deserve to achieve it. Otherwise you will have no commitment to your goal, or, worse, you will sabotage your outcome because you don't believe you deserve the goal.

3 **You must believe that your goal is realistic.** You can change from a downward progression of a limiting or negative belief, to the upward progression of a positive belief when you know that something is possible because someone else has done it. Then it becomes possible for you to achieve your goals, if you believe you can do it (Figure 10.1).

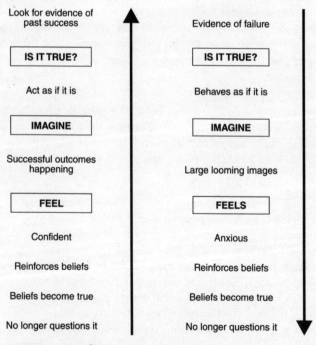

Figure 10.1 The upward progress of a positive belief and the downward progression of a negative

Beliefs, when charged with emotional intensity, become convictions – and spur us to greater actions:

▶ Reframe the context and content of your belief to be positive.

▶ Substitute your belief with evidence of past success.

▶ Act as if your belief is true.

▶ Reinforce your belief with on-going evidence of success.

▶ Often when beliefs become true to us we tend not to question them and this can lead to inflexibility. In order to grow, you must constantly challenge your beliefs.

Changing unhelpful pictures

Case study: Claire

Claire wanted to change her career and work for a stockbroker. On three occasions she had reached the interview stage but had been turned down. She felt that there was an extra piece of information she needed to produce at her interviews if she was to be a serious contender for a job.

Claire knew what she had to do and when she had to do it by (she had an interview the following Wednesday). Yet she couldn't quite get around to doing the task.

Claire said she needed to produce an analysis of the top 100 share price projections for interview, but kept putting it off. As she spoke, her hands seemed to keep pushing an imaginary object down towards her left foot.

'What's the hand gesture about?' I asked.

Claire replied, 'I guess that's me pushing the task away. I don't want to do it, so I keep pushing it away so it stays small and dim and distant down there.' I asked her what would happen if she turned up for interview without the share projections. Claire looked uncomfortable and fell silent.

I asked Claire if she had ever done a similar task well and how was it different from this time. She said that when she had done a task successfully she was motivated and saw the task as 'big and bright and throbbing in intensity, colourful and up close' to her face. And what motivated her? I asked. She realized that it was the fact that others wanted her to succeed at it. (Claire's motivation strategy for doing a similar task successfully was beginning to emerge.) I asked Claire to pretend I was a temp come to fill her role, and to describe what she was 'seeing', 'feeling', 'saying' to herself that motivated her to finish the task successfully.

The main difference between Claire's 'motivated' and 'unmotivated' state was in how colourful and close she pictured the task. She practised switching her demotivating picture from 'small' and 'dim' and 'distant' to seeing it as 'big and bright', 'colourful and up close' to her face. She really felt motivated to do the task now and was able to describe every part of the procedure linked to performing it successfully.

Finally, I asked Claire whether she had a timescale for the completion of her pre-interview task and she said confidently, 'Yes, now I'm motivated to do it. I will complete it by Monday afternoon.'

Changing unhelpful pictures changes motivation:

▷ Change what you 'see', 'hear', 'feel' and 'picture' around performing a task and you will change the way you feel about doing it.

▷ Identify the feeling that comes when you think of performing the unwanted task; often it is a feeling that needs to be changed.

▷ If you can't get around to doing a task you really know you should, ask yourself, 'What are the "pictures" and "feelings" that are demotivating me?'

Focus points

By the end of this chapter you will have:

* Noticed how people become motivated to buy
* Taken a snapshot of your thinking habits and created a blueprint of how you think
* Learned the three parts to changing beliefs
* Noticed your triggers and how you become motivated to make decisions
* Considered changing a habit by looking at what is holding it in place.

Next step

Limiting styles of thinking and behaviour make life more difficult because they can lead to 'stuck' situations. If we can notice and categorize the sort of habitual thinking that may be stopping us from reaching goals, we can replace it with something new that will keep all the benefits of the old habit and still get us the outcome we want.

We could all do with a little support to stay motivated in any task that we do, and the next chapter will give you some tips and tools for *staying* motivated.

11

Stay motivated

In this chapter you will:

- ▶ *Learn that you can't fly with eagles if you are mixing with turkeys*
- ▶ *Discover tips for remaining motivated*
- ▶ *Learn how to put a relapse management strategy in place*
- ▶ *Focus on what is important and not allow other things to get in the way.*

Stay away from negative people – because they will bring you down

'You can't fly with eagles if you are mixing with turkeys.'
Origin unknown

We become like the people we mix with most often. Our aims and ambitions grow or shrink to match those of the people around us. In many TV soaps (at least in the UK) you see negative behaviour mirrored up close. Many of the characters are portrayed as having low ambitions and sink even lower to achieve their aims. A character that seems to be striving hard to better themselves is either derided by others, killed off, or written out of the cast. No one is a winner. Choose the people that you mix with carefully – people who are winners and are actively striving for success. Join a group of similar-minded people; those that will help and mentor each other are best.

If you must spend time with negative people, then ration your time with them to short bursts. Of course, there are times when people genuinely are upset and it is important to be as sympathetic and helpful as you can, but there are people who seem programmed to run a downward cycle of negative thinking whenever they can think out loud in other people's presence. One way to stop them is to derail their downward cycle of negativity and push their positive conversation button.

I have a friend who is a wonderful and most interesting person, but who often runs a broken record of all the negative things he can recount to me. I ask 'How are you?' and this is the cue for the negative stories to begin. I now wait for him to go through a couple of these droning stories before saying 'Yes! And apart from that how are you?' He then flips his thinking to what's good about life, and we have a meaningful and interesting conversation and I realize why that person is still my friend.

Tips for staying motivated

'Believe in yourself, believe in your purpose' is the mantra of the self-motivated. But often it is hard to stay motivated when things are not going to plan. At times like this we need to plumb our inner resources. Here are some tips for people who want to become and stay motivated.

STAY CONNECTED TO OTHER PEOPLE

The way you think determines what you feel. And staying motivated, especially if you are working alone, or are the only motivated person in your vicinity, can mean that you cut yourself off from the people and stimulus you need. It is important to take time out from your project to look around and smell the flowers; otherwise you may find you lose contact with friends.

If you are starting a long project, then tell people in advance. Say: 'I will be busy for a while. I will stay in touch by making the odd phone call and I am really looking forward to having a celebration meal with you at the end of my project.' Planning the event in advance and imagining meeting up again with friends is a way of still feeling connected with them. Knowing that you have already put the wheels in action by stating what you will do to make it happen is also reassuring.

HAVE A RELAPSE MANAGEMENT STRATEGY IN PLACE

When things don't go to plan and you want to feel better ask yourself three questions:

1 'How can I make sense of this thing that has happened?'

2 'What have I learned from it that I can take away and use?'

3 'With hindsight what would I do differently now?'

Develop the habit of analysing and profiting from setbacks so that you build effective feedback loops which you can observe and learn from.

CREATE A 'BUDDY' SYSTEM

Have someone in your corner routing for you. Choose someone who is going through a similar life journey and between you decide on the best way to press each other's 'hot' buttons that will motivate you to do greater things.

These 'whoop-'em-up' conversations are really powerful because, although your best friend might now and again hit upon the words you want to hear, your buddy will do it every time you speak to them.

Case history: Martin and James

Martin and James are friends who ring each other up, each with a list in hand of five specific things they must say to each other during the conversation that the other person wants to hear. Comments may range from 'You are a really excellent public speaker and deserve to be heard worldwide' to 'You have perseverance and I know you will get there.'

HAVE A MISSION STATEMENT AND REVISIT IT OFTEN

When things get tough and you feel your resolve wavering, have pictures and diagrams of what your finished projects will look like. Spend time visualizing in Technicolor your success, the events leading up to it and receiving your reward. Visit your mission statement often and note your progress so that you keep a positive outlook.

Remember this

Have a clear sense of purpose that describes who you are and what you are about. Commit it to memory and recite it like a poem or mantra.

TRACK YOUR PROGRESS

Use gold stars or some other indicator that you can stick on a chart to show your progress to date. Sometimes just seeing how far you have come will be enough to spur you on towards your goals.

DECIDE TO BE HAPPY

Deciding to be happy is a decision that only you can make. Let what makes you happy be a pointer for the direction you take in life. Make happiness your goal and avoid losing yourself in busyness. Stay in touch with yourself and feel for your inner joy. When you are happy, you are creative and all of your talents bubble up and come to the fore.

HAVE A MENTOR AND BE A MENTOR TO SOMEONE

Mentoring will give you a powerful feeling of connection to others. Also, at a skills level, explaining how things work to other people builds your own capabilities. A survey of top UK bosses revealed that 70 per cent of UK males heading UK companies have had at least 12 mentors.

STAY IN TOUCH WITH YOURSELF

Our beliefs are constantly changing in relation to the sights we see and the thoughts and feelings we experience. But sometimes we can get so caught up in busyness that we are not aware of the changes going on within us until something happens that startles us, and we are forced to take time out to re-evaluate our beliefs. Be open and aware of the subtle changes that happen within.

Try it now: Practise early-morning writing

Ask yourself a question about whatever is foremost in your mind, and follow up with ten minutes of really fast writing , to allow whatever is on your mind to tumble out. Let the pen fly down the page followed hastily by your hand.

A phrase by E.M. Forster sums the up technique: 'Think before you speak is criticism's motto. Speak before you think is creation's motto.' Early-morning writing lets you stay in touch with yourself, your goals, your needs, your desires. It also shows you how creative you can be when you are thinking freely.

FOCUS ON WHAT IS IMPORTANT AND DO NOT LET OTHER THINGS GET IN THE WAY

Calmly review your schedule for the last week and decide: what did you really do that is worth mentioning? Allow yourself 20 minutes each day to reflect on how you can use your time doing more of what is of value to you. Decide that in future you will cut out anything that was busyness merely masquerading as something important.

BE FULLY PRESENT WITH PEOPLE

If you are busy, you may not be able to spend a long lunch hour with someone, but you can spend ten minutes. Pick one or two people a day and decide to make the time spent with them special. Show the person that you are listening to them and that what they have to say is of interest to you. Most people do not experience being wholly listened to by another person very often, so this is one of the most powerful things that you can do with someone to build up a shared relationship with deep rapport.

CONGRATULATE YOURSELF

Thinking an occasional thought about how well you have done lately will not do as much good as were you to set it in a frame and make it significant and visible. Write a list of all the things that you have achieved and made happen in the last few months, then read them aloud with gusto and, as you do so, feel really proud. To embed your success, print the achievements of which you are really proud in large letters on A4 paper and stick them inside cupboard doors so you can see them several times a day. Get that feeling of vitality and powerfulness that comes with knowing that you are a person who constantly makes things happen.

MAKE AFFIRMATIONS

Affirmations are a lovely way of focusing on what you have in life, and the things that you want to bring into your daily living. There are thousands to choose from and if you read a book of affirmations you can choose the ones that resonate with you each day.

You can change your affirmations whenever you want to, depending on what you want to draw into your life. Some favourites are: 'I have abundance, joy, love and fulfilment in my life'; 'I am the teacher I never had'; 'I embrace all living creatures, and the whole of nature in its beauty'; 'Thank you for everything that comes into my life'; 'Thoughts become things. When I can see it clearly in my mind, I get to hold it in my hand.'

FIND PEOPLE ON THE SAME JOURNEY AS YOU

I run courses at the City Lit in London on 'NLP and Manifesting Abundance' and there is nothing so exciting as meeting participants and finding out that they are life travellers who have stopped at the same port as you, and are making their way on a similar life journey. Treasure these people. If you are networking, find two people in the room and discover what is special about them and what is important to them. This is one of the best ways to find life-travelling buddies.

DEVELOP A SENSE OF HUMOUR

A sense of humour can often free you and those around you from automatic responses to situations, as this letter from a student to her parents demonstrates:

Dear Mum and Dad,

I'm sorry I haven't written to you for a while, but the fire that engulfed my flat also destroyed all my writing materials.

Fortunately, one of the firemen that helped put the blaze out was a nice young man called Wayne, who kindly let me stay with him in his flat. I do so hope you will like him when you meet him, as we got married last week. I did want it to be a surprise, but as I've started telling you all the good news, you also might as well know that you're about to become grandparents. I'm sure you're both delighted.

Your loving daughter,

Sharon.

PS My flat didn't burn down, I'm not married and I'm not pregnant. But I did fail my maths exam. I hope this puts everything into perspective for you.

KEEP THINGS IN PERSPECTIVE

Do not blow things out of proportion. Something that you might have viewed as a major catastrophe can seem like only an irritation in a week's time. A walk in a cemetery on a sunny day will let you know that nothing really matters that much because we all end up in the same place eventually.

SHOW GRATITUDE

Before getting out of bed each day, ask yourself, 'What was good about yesterday?' You will find something worth while about even the worst of days. Then list all the things that you are grateful for having, and carry the feeling this gives you throughout the day. A quote from Lydia Child says it all: 'Gratitude is the memory of the heart; therefore forget not to say often, I have all I ever enjoyed.'

HAVE A BREATHING MANTRA

As you breathe in, roll your tongue under your top teeth. As you breathe out, bring your tongue down behind your bottom teeth. Hold your hand lightly on your stomach and ensure that this is where your breath is coming from, rather than shallow breathing from high up in your chest. Breathe deeply and repeat your own special words as you breathe 'in' and 'out'.

LEARN TO LIVE IN THE PRESENT

If you look closely at your worst fears, you will find they tend to be of the 'what would happen if' variety. Accept that you will have periods of stress, and work out where your stress level lies. At least 90 per cent of the things we worry about never happen; worrying over whether they will or not will bring a cocktail of stressful hormones spiralling through your body.

HAPPINESS IS SOMETHING TO DO

A Chinese proverb says that 'Happiness is something to do, something to love, and something to look forward to'. Make sure you are working on at least one each of these aspects of yourself to lead to self-fulfilment, and that you plan many more for the future.

Try this: The pink bubble meditation for calm

The pink bubble meditation is a good way of calming yourself when you experience stress triggers.

1 Close your eyes and sigh deeply. Become aware of your body, and gradually relax any tension you may feel in your neck, shoulders, forehead and the rest of your body.
2 Slowly begin to focus on your breathing, how the air is being inhaled and exhaled, in and out of your body. Imagine your mind as a glass full of bubbly pink champagne.
3 Fix your gaze on the champagne and allow any thoughts that come out of it to be encapsulated in a pink bubble that slowly rises and

floats away. The bubbles may be irritations, frets and worries about future circumstances; let them all float away. Encapsulate each thought as it appears, then watch it float away.

Gradually your thoughts will become calmer and you will achieve a still, clearer mind. Take some time to stay in this place and be aware of the stillness and calm.

Focus points

In this chapter you will have:

* ✳ Learned you can't fly with eagles if you are mixing with turkeys
* ✳ Discovered lots of tips for staying motivated
* ✳ Learned how to put a relapse management strategy in place
* ✳ Know now to focus on what is important and don't let other things get in the way.

Next step

Many of our assumptions about our unworthiness, or inability to do things, have been handed down to us in childhood, so they are not even our own beliefs but somebody else's. Yet we may acquire these limiting assumptions about our ability to do things and move through life as if they are our own.

In the next chapter we consider how, by challenging our limiting beliefs, we begin to notice the thoughts that limit us. Then we can start to construct assumptions that give us more freedom.

Challenge limiting assumptions

In this chapter you will:

▶ *Learn to recognize people's limiting assumptions*

▶ *Use the new belief generator to build more positive beliefs*

▶ *Explore issues people deal with before they can walk across hot coals*

▶ *Reflect on who chose your beliefs*

▶ *Use new ways of thinking to transform other areas of your life.*

Case study: Walking with fire

Have you attended a motivation training where you cheered, clapped and nodded your head politely to show just how motivated you were by the training you'd received? Well, suppose as part of your training you then had a chance to go outside and demonstrate just how *really* motivated you felt by walking across hot embers. Would you still pass the motivation test?

The fire walk is motivational training that forces its participants to face their fears and insecurities in the most dramatic of ways.

I joined the sales team of Guardian Appointments, an IT recruitment company, on part of their two-day training course. The company wanted to create a sense of team spirit among its staff. That morning some of the 30 employees still thought it was a joke. But by 7.00 p.m. that evening they would be demonstrating just how motivated they felt from the training they'd received by walking over 15 foot of hot embers burning at 1,425 degrees Fahrenheit!

Interview with Simon Treselyan

Simon Treselyan of Starfire human potential training and development was the team's trainer. He was gently spoken and had a complexion as fresh as a cherub's. However, his looks belied the fact that he was an ex-army 'special forces' interrogator, co-ordinator and operator.

Of the motivational fire walk, Simon said: 'Some of it has been taken from the rites of passage of many civilizations throughout history. The fire walk has been used by Native Americans and Hawaiians as an initiatory rite. Passing through the fire moves them through a portal into manhood. These rituals have been used by mankind for thousands of years and have an historical validity and real meaning for human beings.'

I wondered whether the training appealed to women as much as it did to males. 'Although there is a lot of what could be construed as macho-testosterone stuff going on,' Simon replied, 'it actually brings out more sensitivity in men and more focus in women. Fifty-five per cent of the people on our trainings are women, so they outnumber the men. Women want what the men have always had – career structure, focus, and the ability to make money and determine their own future. And this is a very powerful mechanism to make sure that women can have that.'

What are the core issues that people have to deal with before they will walk across hot coals? 'I believe that the greatest instinct of human being is not survival but to do that which is familiar – like staying in a job or relationship when you know you should get out. Basically, people here are learning how to get from one place to another by moving themselves through difficult circumstances.'

The fire walk dramatically enacts the overcoming of fear and feelings of powerlessness. 'It provides a controlled environment where people can make a dramatic change in their life by moving from "can't do" to having achieved something which they thought was impossible within an incredibly short timespan. Once people have done the fire walk they realize they can take that energy and way of thinking and use it to transform other areas of their life, so they can translate it directly to whatever else they want to change.'

Mental focus and mind storming, goal setting and planning are the core of some of Treselyan's course. But in eight hours, can he really take someone who is bored, lacks discipline or has an aversion to structuring or planning ahead and turn them into a motivated goal-setting individual? 'Yes,' Simon claimed, 'you can do it in an hour, if you use the right tools. If you use boring mediocre tools, then you're not going to make someone highly motivated and highly productive.'

Isn't fire walking dangerous? Don't some people get burned? 'Not usually, but the idea of fire walking is very emotive. No one has died while fire walking, and the most that could happen is that you'll get a slight blister. So people have to overcome the illogical fear they have about fire walking. They think: "Oh my God, I'm going to get burned." Yet many of them are quite happy to do something like abseiling which has a proven track record of killing people. That's why the element of fire walking is so powerful.'

All 20 people who did the walk said it was a brilliant experience. 'Yes, I'm pleased about that, but I am absolutely delighted that ten of those people also said it was a life-changing experience. And I'm gratified that some of the participants changed dramatically after the fire walk and felt capable of achieving much more. I recognize that some people don't want this; they are quite happy to be mediocre because it means that they are never going to be challenged. They're always going to have an excuse for not succeeding. But for those people who actually want to see what they're made of, to be the best that they can be, then I will work with them and make them the best.'

Case history 1: Simon Seward, sales consultant

'From the point of stepping off from grass into the fire I just thought, "Walk across the coals, walk across the coals." It felt like putting my foot in hot water and then coming out again. I could feel the heat and I knew that, if I stopped walking, I would get burned... The point of the course was to show people that there are no boundaries. If you can walk across hot coals, what's so difficult about picking up the phone and calling someone to see if they want to buy your product?'

Case history 2: Toby Myers, senior consultant

'My outlook has changed since doing the fire walk. I was very cynical beforehand and had decided I wasn't going to do it and that I didn't need to do it to prove myself. The thing that swayed me was the "mind over matter" exercises. They were weird, but I saw them work, and at that point I had to open my mind and start listening. The walk itself was a very emotional experience and I have changed some of my beliefs because of it. Before the training I strongly believed that if you were angry you were more determined. But I've learned that, if you are positive and happy, you will do so much better.'

Case history 3: Sue Levy, temp controller

'I was hesitant to start with and thought the fire walk might be something I'd choose to opt out of. But when we did an exercise where I broke a board with my hand I suddenly felt empowered to do a lot more. I didn't think the fire walk was dangerous at all. Immediately afterwards I felt on a high. I call on that experience now if I'm in a tricky situation, because if I could achieve something that was seemingly impossible, then I can go on to bigger and better things.'

We create the life we choose, one choice at a time

Holding negative beliefs about ourselves, our capabilities, the people around us, or how things are in the world can limit our abilities to achieve the successes we dream of attaining in life. What's more, the limiting beliefs we hold about ourselves may not even be our own; many will have been given to us by the people who influenced us in childhood. One reason you should constantly challenge your limiting beliefs.

HAVE YOU CONSTRUCTED YOUR OWN CHAINS?

You may have heard the story of young elephants that are trained for work by being chained in leg irons to trees. After a while they realize that attempting to free themselves is futile and eventually they give up. Although they are later unchained for work and could wander off, they never forget the experience; they do exactly as they are told, becoming docile and controllable. The elephant, 40 times more powerful than its handler, believes it cannot break free and so does not attempt to.

Did you get to choose whether you wanted to own the beliefs you have about yourself, your expectations and abilities in life? Or do you, like the elephant, carry limiting beliefs around like excess baggage with you? Do you intend to carry them with you for the rest of your life?

Have you challenged any of the beliefs that you have been carrying with you for a long time? Beliefs that may get in the way of our achievements could include:

▶ 'I'm stupid/scatter-brained/incompetent/not clever enough.'

▶ 'People like me don't run successful businesses / achieve success.'

▶ 'I don't deserve it.'

▶ 'I'm too old / too young / unqualified.'

▶ 'I don't know how to do it.'

Try it now: Have you previously challenged your limiting assumptions?

If so, what were the results? Think about it and briefly write down in a sentence about what happened when you changed a belief in the past.

✳ What was the old belief you held?
✳ What was the new belief you changed it to?
✳ What was the outcome of you changing your belief?
✳ Write the process down.

Limiting beliefs

Try it now: Examine your beliefs

Think of three people you know who you feel are capable of much more than whatever job or role they play in life. Then list any limiting statements you hear them make about their abilities that reinforce their negative beliefs (e.g. 'I can't do it!', 'It's too difficult for me', 'I'll never get a look in').

Now imagine those people were talking about *you*:

* What might they say are the limiting beliefs you hold that might be stopping you from achieving the successful outcomes you dream of?
* Write down each limiting belief so that you can look at ways to chip at and change those assumptions one at a time to beliefs that will empower you and that will support your aims.

Self-assessment: Recognize your own limiting beliefs

Listed below are some of the commonest beliefs that limit people in their chances of success. Tick any with which you identify. How strongly do you hold this belief? Score yourself 1–10, and add any other beliefs that may have been holding you back from achieving success.

Averse to risk taking. Fear of failure. 'I will not strive for what I want because I might fail.' (___/10)

Feeling undeserving. 'Others can achieve their dreams, but not me. I believe that I don't deserve the things I want in life. I am dependent on what others decide they want to give me. And if they don't, then I go without.' (___/10)

Too old/young/not pretty enough/not clever enough. 'My physical appearance prevents me from getting the things I want in life.' (___/10)

I must put other people's needs before my own. 'I cannot satisfy my own needs and care for other people at the same time. I would not be a good person if I put my own needs before others; that would make me a bad person.' (___/10)

Fear of tall poppy syndrome in others. 'I must not boast about my successes. I do not want people to envy me because I am afraid they might cut me down to their size.'   (___/10)

Poverty mentality. 'I must not take risks. I may lose what I already have, even though what I have does not make me happy, move me on, or seem worth having.'   (___/10)

Fear of commitment. 'I am afraid of being tied down or messing up. So I run away when things get tough. I do not have the staying power to see difficult situations through.'   (___/10)

Insecure and blaming others for the things not achieved. 'I seek other people's approval before I make decisions, because I don't trust myself to make the right choices.' This can translate to: 'I could have succeeded but nobody whom I look to for approval thought I was good enough.'   (___/10)

I must be perfect in everything I do. 'So I leave everything to the last minute, or don't get it done, or finish the task when it is too late and nobody wants the results anymore.' The other extreme of this is: 'I am so perfect that no one measures up to my standards. I wonder why no one comes near me by choice any more.'   (___/10)

'Your playing small does not serve the world.'

Marianne Williamson

Try this: Always challenge your limiting assumptions

Write down your limiting beliefs in a list so you can look at ways to challenge them, one by one, and change them to beliefs that will support your aims. Start with the ones that, if you got rid of them, would have the most impressive impact on what they freed you up to do.

Begin by questioning the familiar. What are some of the messages you receive each day from your thoughts, from the behaviour and words of the people around you. Take one belief and question it.

✻ How long have you held this belief?
✻ Who gave it to you?

Establish where your thoughts deviate

It is vital that you establish at what point your thoughts deviate from truth or fact, possible truth or fact, to one of limiting assumption.

Remember this

Once we convince ourselves that a limiting assumption is a truth we no longer question it. In fact, we look for information to substantiate our belief and exclude all else.

EXCLUDING THE FACTS AND GOING WITH THE ASSUMPTIONS

This occurrence can be seen in appeal cases where the wrong person has been imprisoned. On re-examination it often turns out that, once a likely suspect has been apprehended, the information gatherers shut down on all other possibilities. Similarly, once our thinking becomes derailed, we search only for patterns that match our assumptions – and we find them. We can sometimes believe so strongly that our assumptions are 'truth' that, even when we are shown evidence to the contrary, we may still argue passionately for our limiting beliefs.

RECOGNIZING SELF-LIMITING TALK

Now here's a limiting belief: 'I can't change.' Another one is: 'It's always been done like this', which implies that something cannot be changed because it's always been the same. Changing your thoughts, behaviour and beliefs one at a time and in small ways is often all that is needed to begin to change your limiting beliefs and to start steering your life in a direction that brings success.

Key idea: When did you last change a belief

Your beliefs are not carved in stone: you are constantly changing them throughout your life, based on the incoming information you receive. Can you recall the first time someone told you that Santa Claus wasn't real? What did you do? Most children carry on believing until overwhelming evidence triggers disbelief.

Child star Shirley Temple said she stopped believing in Santa Claus when she was taken to a department store to meet him and he asked her for her autograph. At this point she reasoned that Santa was much to famous to ask anyone for an autograph.

Try it now: Examine the specimens in your Museum of Discarded Beliefs

* What major beliefs did you have when you were younger that you changed over time?
* What were the deciding thoughts that occurred when you changed from believing to no longer believing? Describe them in a sentence.
* What was the evidence that satisfied you that it was safe to send this assumption to your Museum of Discarded Beliefs?
* From what you have learned, what sort of evidence might you require to change one of your existing limiting beliefs?

How do you change beliefs?

An untidy person who wants to tidy up their mess but holds the belief 'I don't know how to tidy up' will find their progress inhibited. A more enabling belief to install, one that generates more options might be: "I take responsibility for my actions and take control of my environment.'

Try it now: New Belief Generator

* What new belief will be the catalyst that launches you in the direction of reaching your goal? Take one of you limiting beliefs and examine it.
* What is the positive opposite to each one of your limiting beliefs?
* Write the sentence down when you've got the answer, because these nuggets of insight will be the most precious things you could ever acquire.

WHAT'S UNDER THE ICE?

Limiting beliefs are like hidden icebergs: 90 per cent of what is going on is below the surface of what people are saying. To raise the belief to the surface, the question to ask is:

'Why is it like that?'

The explanation given might be: 'Because I don't have enough time/money/help.'

To uncover more limitations a good question to ask is:

'How do you know that is true?'

Once more of the belief is revealed, you can ask:

'How does you not having X cause Y?'

The explanation will reveal more hidden limitations. Often, if you can cite an example of someone else who has achieved what they want with similar restrictions, it will be enough to start them thinking about how they might be able to make the change.

Don't forget to ask, too: 'Are you sure about that? Is what you're saying a "truth", a "possible truth" or a "limiting assumption"?'

People often impose rules on themselves and then act as though the rule is really true. Example: 'People like me don't go to university.' A question that cuts through their judgmental thinking is: 'According to whom? Who says that people like you don't go to university?'

Again, if you can cite one instance where someone in their circumstances did what they claim to be unable to do, it is often enough to reignite their thinking processes around how they might overcome their limiting thoughts enough to take action and achieve the things they want.

Case study: Sue

Sue: I want to be an actress, but I can't because I am too old.

Question: How do you know you are too old?

Sue: Because I do – all the actresses you see on television are young.

Question: All of the actresses you see on television are young, every single one?

Sue: Well no, not all of them, but most of them. I just get a feeling that producers want young, sexy actresses.

Question: Everyone, every single producer, wants young, sexy actresses?

Sue: Well no, not every single producer – there are parts that call for older people.

Question: So there are parts that call for older actresses?

Sue: Well yes, a few...

Question: Have you seen any...?

Key idea

Do not allow your brain to make negative statements about you without challenging it to support its purported facts with evidence.

NEVER, EVER

When people imagine a situation to be true in all circumstances they use words like 'always' and 'never' and may generalize a situation that is particular to them as if it applies to everyone.

> *Example:* 'I could never leave my family alone to go to tap-dancing classes. I must always be there when they come home.'

To break the generalization you can repeat the words they use as a question:

> 'You could never leave your family alone, never? Never, ever? Not in any circumstances?

> Not even if you had a baby-sitter?

Not even if you were having another baby and had to go to hospital?'

Letting people see that there are circumstances in which they may break, or might have already broken, their generalized belief about how a situation should be, may be enough to open up their thinking. There is the possibility that there may be situations where it is OK to change their beliefs in order to satisfy their desires.

TAKING RISKS

Often when people are afraid of taking risks it is because they are prone to imagining all the terrible things that could go wrong. Asking them to imagine what things would be like if all went beautifully and according to plan can open up new possibilities in their thinking.

Chronic negative thinkers may argue that they could not even imagine themselves taking a risk, let alone actually doing it. To catch them off-guard ask:

'How would it be if you could imagine taking the action?'

Before a person can respond to this question they have to imagine doing the task. This flips their thinking and they will answer:

'Well, it might be OK.'

At this point ask them to describe the image in more detail. Get them to tell you how they would do the task, and once you are sure that they know what to do, ask:

'And what would doing/getting/being what you want do for you?'

Often this is new territory for people who have never strayed beyond their thinking boundaries, so allow for lots of hesitations, silences and false starts:

'I run away when things get tough / when I'm afraid of committing to an action or person.'

'I do not have the staying power to see difficult situations through.'

Ensure that you have good rapport with the person you ask this question:

> 'So you run away when things get tough? Why is that bad for you?'

The answer might be:

> 'People I look up to might be angry with me.'

Ask the question again:

> 'And what is important about that?'

The answer might be:

> 'I would feel upset because I have let them down.'

Keep asking:

> 'And why would that be bad for you?'

Be prepared to help the person accept the feelings they have uncovered so that they can move on and deal with the problem.

HANKERING AFTER PERFECTION

This can result in procrastination. The person finishes the task when it is too late and nobody wants the results any more.

Everyone has values that are important to them. Asking them,

> 'What is important to you about being perfect in everything you do?'

will give you an idea of the person's values. A possible answer may be:

> 'It's important that I do good work; it's just that I don't seem to be able to get it done on time.'

The question to unstick the person could be:

> 'How would you like to be able to get it done?'

The procrastinator will tell you how to do things on time and list what needs to be changed in order to get things done on time. Feed the information back to them and ask how it would be if they used this process for getting things done on time. If the new strategy feels right, and works for them, they will find it easier to adopt.

The power of presupposing

Presuppositions are beliefs individuals hold about themselves or others, or how they think situations are in the world. We presuppose that these beliefs are true and act as if they are. At one time it was widely believed that the world was flat. If you held that belief now, how would it affect your thoughts on travelling to the underside of the world – say, Australia?

Try it now: Notice how you changed your thoughts

Think of an action that you once believed you couldn't do, but can do now, for example riding a bike, roller-skating, swimming, giving a talk or chairing a meeting. How did you feel before you performed the feat? Did you think you would ever do it? What happened to change your thinking from 'I can't do that' to 'I can do that!'?

Think of something you cannot presently do but would like to do. Ask yourself some questions about the actions you need to be able to do in order to achieve it. People often think in absolutes such as 'I can't do that...' So let's take something that you currently believe you could not do and play with some new questioning strategies to loosen up the language.

Present belief	New question
'I can't do that...'	What would happen if you could?
'I can't do that yet...'	What will happen when you can?

Changing your language and moving from 'I can't do that' (an absolute) to 'I can't do that yet' (which presupposes that you can see a time in the future when you can) offers a glimmer of hope.

Having freed up the questions a little, imagine in detail that you have performed the action and answer this question:

'What did I do differently,

or

'What was different about me that enabled me to do it?'

Key idea

Your brain processes both fact and imagined events as if they are real. This is why you can imagine something sad, make an association and start crying, even though you have not experienced the event.

Try asking yourself some more questions about your capabilities. You might believe:

'I can't give a presentation in front of people.'

Present belief	New question
'It's too difficult.'	What would have to happen for it to be easier?

If you relax and listen, your brain will tell you what you need in order to make the action seem easier:

'It's easier now but...'	And what else would you need to make it even easier than that?

Build success into your future

Have you ever performed a task incredibly well, so well you thought it was achieved by magic? It may have been in school performing a sport, persuading a group of work colleagues to agree to your plan, making a sale to a particularly difficult customer or asking someone for a date. The following exercise will enable you to use this experience to help create future success.

Try it now: Freeze-frame your achievements

When the event occurred...

* Did it feel as if you were playing your part with ease?
* Had you prepared for the event and rehearsed it in your mind?
* Were you purposeful in your thoughts, beliefs and behaviour?

In the above example, you believed in yourself and that you would do whatever you set out to do. The vision of your success is stored in your imagination and body, and you can imagine the event by playing it back in your mind. You may see the event in colour, like watching a movie, and recall each frame in sequence.

If you took all your past memories and images of success, and the pictures and strong emotional feelings that are tied up with them, and you carried these successful beliefs about your capabilities into the future – what sort of things might you be capable of achieving if you knew that you simply could not fail?

Try it now: Create beliefs that build success

1 Write down a limiting belief that may have held you back from success in the past. What do you believe is the positive opposite of that belief – one that would lead you to outstanding success?
2 What limiting beliefs do you want to remove now, so that you can move towards your next success?
3 If you were going to take the first step in challenging one of these limiting beliefs, what would that first step be?

Getting rid of just one of your limiting thoughts about your capabilities will let you dispose of excess mental baggage and will help you to focus on the things you really want in life. As your confidence builds and you are recognized as a motivated person, you will become more attractive to others both financially and emotionally, because people are attracted to confident people with positive energy.

Remember this

By building your level of motivation you can make a difference to what you can achieve in the world. Once you successfully obtain the results you want from life every day, your sense of fulfilment and satisfaction will increase and your confidence to reach greater goals will grow.

Acting as if you are already what you want to become, and knowing that you can become that person, is the way to remove self-doubt and enter your real magic kingdom.

Focus points

In this chapter you will have:

- Explored issues people deal with before they can walk across hot coals
- Learned to recognize people's limiting assumptions
- Used the New Belief Generator to build more positive beliefs
- Reflected on who chooses your beliefs.

Next step

Motivation is about having the confidence to act on your dreams. It is about knowing how to take energy and ways of thinking and use them to transform your life. In the next chapter we will explore some more powerful tips and strategies for your personal toolkit. We will learn how you have the ability to expand your thinking at will. We will also develop your listening skills.

13

Learn modelling strategies

In this chapter you will:

▶ *Learn that you have the ability to expand your thinking at will*

▶ *Formulate questions that elicit other people's successful strategies*

▶ *Acquire some incremental skills that move you closer to your goals*

▶ *Develop your listening skills.*

Modelling other people's strategies

Modelling lets you take an impression of someone else's thinking-through patterns and apply it to your own situation if you are stuck, or need bigger or better solutions than those available to you now. It gives you the power to expand your thinking on a situation at will.

If you can work out how another person can do something that you yearn to do, it opens up a world full of possibilities for you. Knowing that you can observe, map and reproduce the strategies people use to become masters in their fields gives you a blueprint for success. You can model the skills of the most talented people around you and use these skills to achieve your personal goals and desires in life.

Remember this

By modelling what works for other people, you can explore a variety of different strategies that get successful results for other people, and decide which ones you will make your own.

If you're in sales, human resources, training, or any business that requires advanced communication skills you can capitalize on the magic of understanding how people do the things they do. Get the action habit – you don't need to wait until conditions for learning new skills are perfect. Whenever you see somebody with a really good skill, one that you'd like to acquire, get into the habit of asking, 'How do you do that?'

Knowing what motivates other people to make their choices can help you change your life to be just the way you want it. Suppose you want to be slim, trim and active: you could model a range of slim people's thinking and behaviour and find out what it is about their strategies that keeps them slim. Ask them how *they* decide when it is time to eat.

Similarly, if you want to be a successful entrepreneur, spend an evening at a gathering of entrepreneurs and build up a picture of what makes them different from the rest of the herd.

Entrepreneurs tend to be proactive, they make decisions quickly and are also prepared to take the sort of risks other people might not. They tend to think big and aim high.

Self-assessment: How do you score as a high achiever?

To find out how you score as a high achiever, for each of the statements below rate yourself on a scale of 1–10.

1 High achievers have a passion for what they are doing.   (__/10)

2 They feel passionately about their goals.   (__/10)

3 They believe their actions can make a difference.   (__/10)

4 They believe that life is about seizing chances and learning from experiences.   (__/10)

5 Their goal is overcoming challenges.   (__/10)

6 They have the ability to observe, identify and adapt other people's strategies for their own uses.   (__/10)

7 Their energy and enthusiasm comes from being on purpose and working towards their goals.   (__/10)

8 Successful people are master communicators.   (__/10)

Check your scoring in the boxes and for each topic spend 60 seconds thinking about what new technique in this area you could acquire that would increase your score and help you achieve the outcome you want.

Write you list of action points down and prioritize them in order of which new skills will give you most options and leverage towards reaching your goal.

Once you commit to improving your skill, talents and abilities, you can increase your score for any of the above.

Spot the people with talent

What sort of skills could you use that would motivate you and enhance your beliefs about your abilities or advance your career and take you to the top? You don't have to reinvent the wheel and come up with totally original ideas. Start mining the attributes you see in the people around you, initially learning skills that are relatively easy to acquire.

There will be people all around you who are displaying some of the skills you would like to acquire. Observe your colleagues and isolate particular skills you might like to have. Don't pick anything too difficult because you are learning a process at present. Some simple, easy and worthwhile skills to acquire from the people around you might be:

- how to make good decisions
- techniques for solving problems
- drawing spider diagrams to aid your creativity
- taking control of a situation
- how to ask for help
- how to say 'no'
- handling interruptions
- tips for saving time
- chairing successful meetings
- structuring reports
- speed-reading techniques
- organizing your email system
- asking precision questions
- listening for what is really important
- dealing with a cluttered desk
- how to organize yourself
- planning situations in advance
- dealing with the unexpected.

 Try it now: Choose small skills that are easy to acquire

Choose six small practice skills that you really want to acquire from your colleagues. Acquiring these skills will make a visible difference to your overall performance at work. The question to ask to elicit people's strategy for doing the things they do well is 'How do you do that?' Then sit back and listen. Make sure you get the whole procedure – from before they started, to when they finished the strategy.

Remember this

The more we know about how a person demonstrates the kind of excellence we want to have, the easier it becomes to follow their way of working and incorporate their strategies into our working life. Simple physical, observable skills are easiest to start with to learn and practise the process. Modelling shows us that it is not simply an accident, or good luck, that some people can do some things exceptionally well while others find it difficult. Modelling an excellent practitioner is a wonderful way to learn.

Easy skills to acquire

▶ **Find anything fast** How does a colleague in a busy environment manage to lay their hands on a memo, document or anything that is required by a telephone enquirer immediately? If you have got a strategy for this, then it is easy; if you do not have a strategy, then it is worth acquiring. Look around you and see which of your colleagues already has this skill, then find out how they do it. A successful strategy may involve labelling files and putting contents lists on front covers.

▶ **Tidy desk** How does someone with lots of different aspects to their job manage to keep their desk tidy, despite lots of interruptions that draw their attention to other things? If you already have this skill, you may think, 'So what, I do that already.' If you do not have this skill, then it might be a quick and easy strategy to learn. You will reap rewards in that the payoff for acquiring it will be immediate, and you will use the strategy for the rest of your life.

▶ **Where did I leave off?** Many people write lists and notes to themselves to remind them of what they have to do next. However, last-minute bag, purse, trouser or plan changes can leave them bereft of their to-do list. One of the simplest ways of ensuring that you have your list to hand in any situation is at the end of the day to write a to-do list and email it to yourself for the following day. A simple strategy, but see how much it changes the way you work and feel, knowing that you already know what you have to do today.

▶ **Staying calm** If you are good at staying calm in a difficult situation, ignore this. If you become flustered and you would like to find a simple strategy for remaining calm, then this would be a really good strategy to learn from a colleague. The benefits of learning this strategy (if you do not already have a successful one) are that you can put it into use immediately and use it every day, which will also increase your confidence.

 Try it now: Stay calm strategy

Repeat the mantra 'calm' and breathe deeply, then go through the following thought processes slowly:

1 Focus on the situation. Collect your thoughts. (Imagine yourself on a seashore slowly and calmly collecting shells, each of which represents a thought, and putting them into a basket.)

2 Seek advice from anyone else if you need to. If you are dealing with a telephone caller, tell them you will call them back.

3 Deal with it. Take the action necessary to resolve the situation.

This is a very simple strategy. Practise it a few times to find out whether it does or does not work for you. Notice how colleagues around you who are good at becoming 'calm' do it, and become curious about their different strategies. Find two or three different ways for doing 'calm' and practise each to see which one works best for you.

▶ **'Do it now' fever.** You may have a colleague who, when given a task, takes off like a whippet at the starting gate to complete it. If you are not as highly motivated, but would like to be, it may be worth noticing what is happening when this person is given a command. If you are a person who thinks, 'Do I really need to do this task? Is it absolutely necessary? I will sit on it for a day or two to think it through,' then get curious enough to ask your colleague 'What do you think when you are given a new task? How do you do what you do?' Find out what is going on mentally and physically for them when they are given a new task to perform. Notice particularly, and write down, the beliefs they hold about doing tasks straight away.

Make it a habit to be curious about how people around you get the successful results you want to have, and then begin to acquire these simple new strategies in every area of your life. Think about which strategies would enhance your performance, then find people who are already demonstrating these skills. What are these people thinking and doing when they perform a task really well? Study their process from beginning to end, then capture the essence and make it your own.

Acquiring small incremental skills, like the everyday ones that are being performed well all around you, can change your performance from average to outstanding. If you become proficient at a dozen new strategies, you are much more likely to be noticed and to accelerate your career path.

Once you are confident in acquiring simple, easily found skills, it is time to move on to eliciting strategies that require greater focus on your part, ones that will begin to markedly improve your performance – and ultimately change your daily experience to that of being a successful performer in every aspect of your life.

Case study: Frances Coombes – even your fingers can be flexible

When I felt twinges of RSI in my wrist I decided to model the skills of someone who wrote equally well with both hands, so I could lessen the strain on my left arm. Finding an ambidextrous person who had acquired the skills in adulthood was difficult but also illuminating. James, an architect, had broken his right arm at university and taught himself to write fluently with his left hand in order to gain his degree.

I asked James to imagine the first time he had written automatically with his non-dominant hand and to re-enact the process. By modelling his behaviour and sensory processes around writing, I discovered that the quickest way to master hand control and writing legibly was from a standing position. The body weight should be evenly balanced on both legs to give a feeling of being grounded, and for poise and control of the pen. The writing surface, I discovered, should be at kitchen surface level, or some convenient height to aid writing in an upright position.

I had never heard of such a writing strategy before, yet as I listened to James I was struck by how obvious it seemed.

I set myself the goal of practising ten minutes each morning for 30 days, writing for either clarity, speed or flow. Within a month I could write fluently with either hand. I now maintain my new habit by spending two minutes a day writing to-do and shopping lists while standing up.

Remember this

If someone else can do something that you want to, then find that successful person and model him or her and how they do it. Modelling becomes exciting once you realize that a skill that might have taken months to learn can be acquired in a very short time.

Eliciting a strategy

As we have seen, if you want to enhance your performance in any sphere, then the best way to do this is to model the behaviour of the people around you who already possess these skills. But what is the best way to elicit their strategy, so that you can understand it inside out, so to speak?

There are three things to look for when modelling someone's strategy:

1 What are their beliefs that support the skill they are doing? Listen for words and phrases like 'I believe', 'I think', 'it's important that…' These words indicate that whatever they say directly afterwards is important to that person and it is what they believe.

2 Pay attention to how their body language and demeanour changes as they recount or run their strategy. Notice any change in their manner, posture and the way they hold themselves as they begin to relate their account and associate with the task.

3 Notice at what point the strategy begins and ends. Once you have the person's strategy and know what makes them feel confident and competent about their abilities around it, you need to try on their beliefs.

When rehearsing the strategy, sit or stand as they did and adopt their body postures. Run through the strategy yourself, saying it out loud as you perform it. Repeat whatever your model has told you in precisely the same language they used. They will be able to correct you if anything is wrong because you have plucked this strategy from their world and the slightest mistake you make will jar with them.

At this point you should have acquired the strategy. If you run it through and nothing happens for you, ask the person to do it again and talk it through – something may be missing.

Sometimes when people are so familiar with a process that it becomes a habit, there are parts of it that are so obvious to them that they fail to explain them. More often than not, the missing part is the crucial piece of information that you need to make sense of how the strategy works.

Run through the strategy several times until you know you've got it and then practise using it for a few days. Decide whether the beliefs that this person holds around their strategy fit well with your own beliefs before deciding to adopt their strategy.

Try it now: Elicit a strategy

1 Ask the person to carry out or re-enact the behaviour.
2 Find out the very first thing the person is aware of as they enter the cycle of behaviour.
3 Note which sensory representation system they are using to enter the loop by listening for 'I see', 'I hear', 'I feel', 'I need to'. This will tell you the initial state the person needs to be in to start the process. If they need to be prompted, then ask:
   ▷ 'Did you see an image in your mind's eye?'
   ▷ 'Did you say something to yourself like "That's a job well done"?'
   ▷ 'Did you have a feeling about it?'
   ▷ 'Are you triggered by something internal or external? Do you here an inner voice, a memory or feeling?'
4 Ask the person what they noticed next (picture, sound, feeling), and again identify the sensory representations. Keep asking the question, 'Was there anything you were aware of before that?' until the person's description of their strategy appears. Carry on until you get the complete sequence of thoughts, pictures, feelings and actions that the person runs to perform this task.

(Adapted from my article 'Modelling Success Strategies', *Positive Health* magazine, issue 120, February 2006, www.positivehealth.com/author/ frances-coombes/frances-coombes)

Case study: Janette

Janette did a lot of research reading for work and wanted to find a way of distilling the essence of what was in the books. She chose three people to model who were excellent at this skill.

Through modelling these people she discovered that: 'They all thought systemically at a very basic level. They believed that all information was connected and part of a bigger picture.' Detachment and objectivity seemed to be key to all three people's strategies.

'If they are distilling information from a book, the people all hold the information in a map within their senses and they'll create a picture of the issue, and come up with a premise. So they'll think, "OK, so this is what this is about."

'One person said their picture was a "spider" with tentacles where different sorts of information was held. Another person said their picture was "almost like a globe of the world". There were bits where they would say, "This fits into this and that into that." So as they're going through a meeting or book, what they're doing is looking for connections and relationships to their own internal model.'

Remember this

Think about using modelling when you...

* want to be able to repeat a past performance when you have done something well and do not know how you've done it (self-modelling)
* want to learn a new skill or improve an existing one
* meet someone who is exceptionally good at a particular skill or talent and you want to find out more about how they do it
* want to emulate other people's successes
* want to change parts of what you have done, which might not have been successful, and keep the other parts that worked well.

Listening skills

Ultimately, your goals will be achieved with the help of other people, so you need to develop good communication, persuasion and listening skills.

How well do you listen? Paul Burns, Organization Development Consultant and Psychotherapist, uses the Psychology of Mind (POM) model to show the different stages of listening we go through when someone is telling us something:

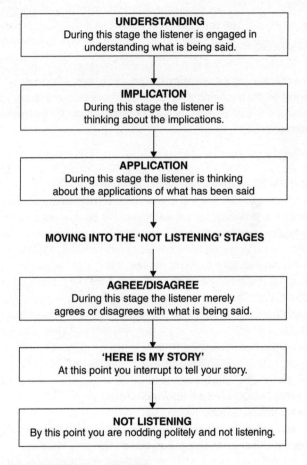

UNDERSTANDING
During this stage the listener is engaged in understanding what is being said.

IMPLICATION
During this stage the listener is thinking about the implications.

APPLICATION
During this stage the listener is thinking about the applications of what has been said

MOVING INTO THE 'NOT LISTENING' STAGES

AGREE/DISAGREE
During this stage the listener merely agrees or disagrees with what is being said.

'HERE IS MY STORY'
At this point you interrupt to tell your story.

NOT LISTENING
By this point you are nodding politely and not listening.

Figure 13.1 The POM stages of listening

Much of what we learn from other people when we talk to them does not come from listening to the actual words they use; we scent it with our whole being.

Remember this

In studies done at the University of Texas to assess the personality traits of 2,000 managers, it was found that, without exception, senior executives scored higher than middle managers when it came to listening and thinking intuitively.

LISTENING TO IGNITE THE MIND

Part of what is termed intuition comes from people's ability to listen and take in information in ways that may seem almost magical to other people who do not possess the same degree of listening skills. Everything we do depends on the quality of the thinking we do first.

Try it now: Explore different listening levels

1 Spend five minutes listening to a friend recounting an experience. You job is to listen and not interrupt, just keep nodding and keep your attention directed at the person in order to keep the conversation going.
2 Afterwards, run through their conversation in your mind and think about what was happening to you as you were listening to that person.
3 Did you stay focused on what they were saying? Or did your attention slip through the different levels of listening?
4 Decide before the next conversation you have with someone that you are going to listen to this person in an understanding way, then see how easy or difficult this is for you.

IMPROVE THE QUALITY OF YOUR LISTENING:
QUANTUM LISTENING

Everything we do in life is affected by the quality of our thinking. And our thinking depends on the quality of our attention for one other. Quantum listening is listening at every level, paying attention to what is happening inside us, maybe noticing that our stomach is a bit tense. You're paying attention to your internal self-talk and what is happening around you. You check out your assumptions but you allow the intuitive process to happen and you notice any subtleties.

Try this: Improve your listening skills

1 Make a stream-of-consciousness recording into a tape recorder by talking out loud. Just say whatever comes into your head and notice how random and non-sequential your thoughts are. Doing this a few times makes you aware of the internal chatter inside you, which can make it difficult to listen attentively to other people.

2 If you have the urge to interrupt someone, make sure that the interruption is preceded by a recap such as 'Let me just check I understand what you are saying', rather than just jumping in and making assumptions. This gives the person a chance to say 'No, I didn't say that', and it gives you a chance to reflect. It also lets people know that, even if you are going to interrupt and counter what they have said, you have heard and understood them and are including them in your thinking process.

Focus points

By the end of this chapter you will have:

* Learned that you have the ability to expand your thinking at will
* Learned that, if a strategy can be described, it can be taught and learned
* Learned to formulate questions that elicit other people's successful strategies
* Acquired some incremental skills as leverage toward achieving your goals.
* Developed your listening skills.

Next step

The creative part of modelling requires you to stretch your thinking by taking on the beliefs, physiology and strategies of another person performing a skill you'd like to acquire and adapting it for your own uses.

Identifying new strategies gives you incredible powers to move beyond what you may have previously considered to be your limits. Once you have acquired your new skills and built them into your neurology so that they become part of your regular behaviour, you develop almost magical powers to attract the things you want into your life.

The next chapter looks at the possibilities of what will happen when you combine all your new learning, tools, tips and behaviours together.

14

Take the leap!

In this chapter you will:

▶ *Learn to recognize opportunities when they appear*

▶ *Check your toolkit for your journey – do you have what you require?*

▶ *Understand how important it is that you achieve the life you desire.*

Fortune favours the prepared

Case study: Stuart

Stuart was a teacher but had always burned to be a rock music journalist. He kept the day job and waited for the call. He submitted some sample reviews to the editor of a well-known rock magazine. The editor liked the writing style and offered Stuart a commission. Unfortunately, the news arrived at the worst possible moment: Stuart was tutoring schoolgirls for their A level exams when the school secretary popped her head round the classroom door and laughed hysterically. 'Stuart, there's a rock magazine on the phone,' she said. 'They want you to pack your bags and fly to Canada to cover a gig on Saturday.' In Stuart's own words: 'It did no harm.' He is now a rock journalist and writes regular reviews for the music press.

When situations move fast, as in Stuart's case, it can feel like you are standing in a railway station waiting for a train. You don't know when it's coming; you don't know where it will be going. But you're standing on the platform with your toolkit packed ready for whatever happens. Suddenly a train roars in. You have no time to think, you get on board and within seconds the doors close and you are off in a totally new direction. Your life has changed, for ever. At times like these there is no time to stop and reflect on the groundwork you prepared that led you to this life-changing event. Be grateful for the abundance that has come into your life, and be prepared to reap your rewards.

You have acquired skills and resources to help you handle whatever comes your way. It is important at this stage that you have a plan for the life you want to lead and that you keep your toolkit open and ready so that you can see the range of strategies that are available to you. You don't need to know all of the specifics of how you will achieve your desires in life. Once you know the general direction you are going in, then the universe opens up for you, and often in unexpected ways.

When you are clear about what is important to you, your beliefs, values and goals align and you will be drawn to doing things that express who you are in a meaningful way. At this point you become a self-organizing system that is in flow. Your ducks are lined up in a row! You will recognize opportunities when they start to appear and achieve your aims almost magically. A chance remark, a change in economic climate, a casual conversation with a stranger, may be enough to take your life in a totally different direction.

Try it now: Check your toolkit

What skills have you already acquired, and what new tools do you need to learn, that will help you to achieve your dreams? Circle the resources that you will use to get the outcome you want.

STRATEGY	RESOURCES	FLEXIBLE THINKING	INFORMATION GATHERING
Use Principles for Success model – begin with your end in mind.	Visualize the best outcome – what will you be seeing, hearing, saying to yourself when you have success?	Plan your well-formed outcome: Is it SMART (Specific, Measurable, Achievable, Realistic, what is the Timescale?)	Seeing other viewpoints – gain insight into situation, gather information, build flexible thinking.
Manage your internal state – be at cause in your life, not at the effect of other people.	Choose a better metaphor for life, one that works for you – e.g. 'Life is like an orchestra, and I am the conductor.'	Use other people's successful thinking strategies to help you think massively outside of the box.	Explore your values – they are what motivate you to achieve the things you want in life.
Problem solving – challenge limiting assumptions to help you move on and reframe limiting beliefs.	Recognize people's thinking patterns, to communicate well, build rapport and negotiate with others.	'I have all the resources I need. If someone else can..., so can I.' Elicit their strategy!	Gather your resources and build your own skills bank. What other tools do you observe that are available to you?
Use other people's thinking strategies – seeing how others are lets you try on and generate new solutions.	Chunk your thinking up or down – useful for negotiating (chunk up for agreement; chunk down for specifics).	Challenge limiting beliefs to help yourself and others move on when blocked.	Notice what motivates you to get things done, then build these things into your achievement strategy

* Write a sentence on how owning each of these skills, and making them your own, will motivate you and give you leverage towards achieving your outcome.
* Practise using at least one resource from your toolkit each day so that the type of thinking each uses becomes automatic.

Remember this: Be prepared for whatever happens

Once you have a dream, identify the tools and techniques you will need to achieve it. Then hone your skills so that you are ready for the call when it comes.

> 'You are your own Devil, you are your own God.
> You fashioned the paths your footsteps have trod.'
>
> Tieme Ranapiri, Maori poet

How important is it that you achieve the life you desire?

Your level of motivation will determine how committed you are and whether or not you will reach your goal.

Self-assessment: How committed are you to being your most successful?

Answer each question, rating yourself on a scale of 1–10.

1 How committed are you to being successful at whatever you do and are you prepared to raise your standards in order to get it? (___/10)

2 Do you have an unshakeable belief that you can get whatever you set out to achieve in life? (___/10)

3 Are you mentally equipped with the tools and problem-solving techniques that you need to deal with any challenges? (___/10)

4 Are you flexible enough to tailor your strategies to get the results you desire? (___/10)

5 In short, do you know what to do, the order you need to do it in, and how to apply your whole focus to achieving your goals? (___/10)

Try it now: Boost your leverage

1 For each of the questions above, ask yourself: 'What actions would I need to take to increase my score by another 2 or 3 points?'
2 When you've discovered the actions you need to take, then ask: 'What is the next step I can take in this area that will give me leverage towards my outcome.'
3 Then, using the SMART technique, write down how you will put your plans into action and then resolve to take action.

 Remember this

You can speed up your development by identifying the key skills of the people who are good at these things. Modelling requires that you identify the behaviours, skills and capabilities, and beliefs they hold that make them so good at what they do. Incorporate those types of behaviours into your own.

Know how much control you have over a situation

In any situation you undertake calculate how much control you have over it, using a three-circle model of control:

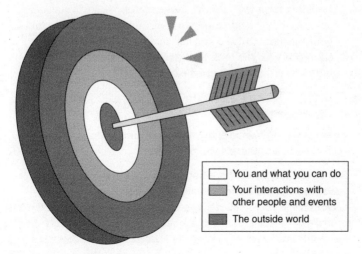

☐ You and what you can do

▨ Your interactions with other people and events

■ The outside world

Figure 14.1 The three-circle model of control

- The **inner circle:** these are the things you can make happen.

- The **middle circle:** these are things that you can initiate and have some control over.

- **The outer circle:** this is the wider context – you can put your idea out into the universe so that people know about it, yet you are ultimately dependent on outside factors.

Let's take the simple example of a plan to buy a new car:

- If you have the means to pay for it, then the choice is totally yours, so that goal fits in your inner circle, because you have 100-per-cent choice.

- If you have to consult other people, say your bank manager, partner or parents, then the outcome depends partly on how you conduct yourself in negotiations with others. You cannot wholly predict the outcome but by conducting yourself well when you interact with others you can influence what happens. You might have 20- to 70-per-cent control of the outcome.

- The outside circle consists of what is happening in the outside world, the things you don't have control over. You may, for example, want a particular model but it may not be available for a few months. Nevertheless, you can set some intentions and send your ideas out into the world. Dream of your passions daily so you can make sure you are already equipped with the tools and techniques required to operate in this area when you get the call.

Remember this

Two of the most powerful tools you have in your personal armoury are your ability to set goals and to model skills.

You cannot control the future or decide what you will be doing five years from now when success knocks on your door, but you can decide on the next small steps you will take today and tomorrow to make the success you want a reality. Get motivated – start increasing your skills and taking the actions that make successes happen more quickly.

Hold your vision steadfastly in your mind's eye

To be passionately engaged in your dreams, you need to hold your vision steadfastly in your mind and see yourself being successful at everything you do. You also need to increase your level of achievement and observable successes in your everyday life.

Three things will help you here:

1 **Modelling successful role models.** Get into the habit of asking people, 'How do you do that?' Find out and then assess that person's strategy, its effectiveness and limitations.

2 **Understanding thinking styles,** your own and other people's.

3 **Assessing the feedback you get from the things you do.** If something you are doing is not working, then try something else. Change your pattern of behaviour until you get the results you want.

Align your beliefs and values

When the actions and behaviour we follow support our deepest needs and we are free from internal conflict, we produce our most magical results. Once you know what excites and motivates you and you are prepared to take the actions to make your dreams a reality, then you will magically move towards your purpose.

Now you need a procedure for standing back and scrutinizing your ideas to know whether the goals you seek are attainable and within what period of time. Remember the SMART strategy.

Remember this

Success means different things to different people. Someone else might see success as having the energy, fitness and body of an athlete; another person might see success as creating something unique, having a millionaire lifestyle or a loving relationship. Another person might see their success as helping others and making a difference to people's lives. However you define your success, you then need to make a plan and impose an order on it (see Chapter 3)

It is vital that you create a well-formed outcome for every project you intend to start. Rank your goals by their level of importance to you. Make sure that you are not deflecting your energy by focusing on too many goals. Some will be distractions that will never come to fruition, and they will divert some of your attention from the things you really do want to achieve.

Follow your passions

What do you feel passionate about? What do you burn to do? What would you do if money were no object and you could do anything in the world you wanted to do?

Remember this

When creating ideas, remember the Walt Disney Dreamer/Realist/Critic strategy (see Chapter 6).

Try it now: Challenge yourself

Pick one big, possibly scary, goal that you yearn to achieve. You may have been nursing your idea for a while but have never thought it through completely.

1 Allow yourself the luxury of spending a week thinking about this big idea and just letting it grow and grow. Do not put boundaries around your thinking – let the ideas build and explode in your mind. Keep a notebook to write down your ideas as they come and do not censor anything.
2 Then go back a week later as a realist and spend some more time asking, 'What would have to happen for these ideas to work for me?'
3 Comb through your ideas picking out the nuggets and discarding the sludge. You may have come up with a completely different idea by now and have moved on to something more realistic. That is how many people make great leaps towards and achieve the things they have always wanted to achieve.

Increasing your motivational drives and enhancing your performance

Do you believe that you could raise your standards and become 10 per cent or even 20 per cent better at any of the topics covered? Of course you could! We can all become better in any areas on which we focus our attention. The trick is to know the order in which to do things so that you can become systematically more powerful in your thinking, action planning and completion drives.

Try it now: Gathering your resources – capture a feeling

Remember when you did something really well, something that made you feel really proud...

* What were the beliefs you held about your abilities to achieve your aim?
* What sort of things did you say to yourself about the thing you were achieving?
* Was your motivation drive high?

Recall that feeling every morning, harness it and carry it with you for the day.

Remember, in everything that's really important to us – love, life, friendship, success – feelings come first. We may spend our school life learning about logic, but all the really big decisions we make in life, such as whom we marry, where we live, and what we want from life, are made with our emotions.

> 'The feelings come before the actions. Therefore you need to be finely attuned to your feelings. When your feelings and whole attention are focused on your goal, you can attain it, providing you know the syntax for success – which is the order of how you do things.'
>
> Martin Goodyer, motivational trainer of
> Reach International Associates

Take the leap! Your action plan for success

RAISE YOUR STANDARDS

Whatever your standard is now, whether it's good or bad, is not relevant; it just is. Whatever you have in life, you have got everything you deserve because the actions you have taken to date have produced it. These are the standards that you have set for yourself up until now, and until you do something different you will not get a different result. Only when you raise that standard yourself can you expect to raise your expectations.

HAVE AN UNSHAKEABLE BELIEF

Raising your standards is not enough. You need to have an absolutely unshakeable belief that says: 'I know I can do it.' If you do not have that, you get a little voice in your head that says, 'Who are you kidding? You've never done it before. Why are you going to do it now? What makes you think you're going to do it now?' The voice in your head is like a little devil that follows you around. You have to banish your little devil, or at least dumbfound him so that he doesn't have anything to say.

KNOW WHAT TO DO AND APPLY IT

Remember a time when you were able to do things that you didn't think you were able to do before. Where did you find the inspiration for doing these things successfully? Look around you now and when you see people with skills you'd like to acquire, ask them, 'How did you do that?'

When you find simple strategies that work, collect them and use them. There is a way of doing most things and you need to have a simple strategy that gives you the right order for the process to work. While there is nothing new in this world, when we do things in a very specific order, we can create magical results.

You now have the resources you need. As your thoughts, plans and actions flow together, your energy grows because you are doing what you love doing. You are focused on creating the destiny you want. You have the tools, you have the motivation, you feel powerful – take the next step and may the force be with you as you journey towards your biggest and best ever goals.

Index

The Way to Write for Television